The New Freedom

A Call For the Emancipation of the Generous Energies of a People

Woodrow Wilson

# THE OLD ORDER CHANGETH

There is one great basic fact which underlies all the questions that are discussed on the political platform at the present moment. That singular fact is that nothing is done in this country as it was done twenty years ago.

We are in the presence of a new organization of society. Our life has broken away from the past. The life of America is not the life that it was twenty years ago; it is not the life that it was ten years ago. We have changed our economic conditions, absolutely, from top to bottom; and, with our economic society, the organization of our life. The old political formulas do not fit the present problems; they read now like documents taken out of a forgotten age. The older cries sound as if they belonged to a past age which men have almost forgotten. Things which used to be put into the party platforms of ten years ago would sound antiquated if put into a platform now. We are facing the necessity of fitting a new social organization, as we did once fit the old organization, to the happiness and prosperity of the great body of citizens; for we are conscious that the new order of society has not been made to fit and provide the convenience or prosperity of the average man. The life of the nation has grown infinitely varied. It does not centre now upon questions of governmental structure or of the distribution of governmental powers. It centres upon questions of the very structure and operation of society itself, of which government is only the instrument. Our development has run so fast and so far along the lines sketched in the earlier day of constitutional definition, has so crossed and interlaced those lines, has piled upon them such novel structures of trust and combination, has elaborated within them a life so manifold, so full of forces which transcend the boundaries of the country itself and fill the eyes of the world, that a new nation seems to have been created which the old formulas do not fit or afford a vital interpretation of.

We have come upon a very different age from any that preceded us. We have come upon an age when we do not do business in the way in which we used to do business,—when we do not carry on any of the operations of manufacture, sale, transportation, or communication as men used to carry them on. There is a sense in which in our day the individual has been submerged. In most parts of our country men work, not for themselves, not as partners in the old way in which they used to work, but generally as employees,—in a higher or lower grade,—of great corporations. There was a time when corporations played a very minor part in our business affairs, but now they play the chief part, and most men are the servants of corporations.

You know what happens when you are the servant of a corporation. You have in no instance access to the men who are really determining the policy of the corporation. If the corporation is doing the things that it ought not to do, you really have no voice in the matter and must obey the orders, and you have oftentimes with deep mortification to co-operate in the doing of things which you know are against the public interest. Your individuality is swallowed up in the individuality and purpose of a great organization.

It is true that, while most men are thus submerged in the corporation, a few, a very few, are exalted to a power which as individuals they could never have wielded. Through the great organizations of which they are the heads, a few are enabled to play a part unprecedented by anything in history in the control of the business operations of the country and in the determination of the happiness of great numbers of people.

Yesterday, and ever since history began, men were related to one another as individuals. To be sure there were the family, the Church, and the State, institutions which associated men in certain wide circles of relationship. But in the ordinary concerns of life, in the ordinary work, in the daily round, men dealt freely and directly with one another. To-day, the everyday relationships of men are largely with great impersonal concerns, with organizations, not with other individual men.

Now this is nothing short of a new social age, a new era of human relationships, a new stage-setting for the drama of life.

---

In this new age we find, for instance, that our laws with regard to the relations of employer and employee are in many respects wholly antiquated and impossible. They were framed for another age, which nobody now living remembers, which is, indeed, so remote from our life that it would be difficult for many of us to understand it if it were described to us. The employer is now generally a corporation or a huge company of some kind; the employee is one of hundreds or of thousands brought together, not by individual masters whom they know and with whom they have personal relations, but by agents of one sort or another. Workingmen are marshaled in great numbers for the performance of a multitude of particular tasks under a common discipline. They generally use dangerous and powerful machinery, over whose repair and renewal they have no control. New rules must be devised with regard to their obligations and their rights, their obligations to their employers and their responsibilities to one another. Rules must be devised for their protection, for their compensation when injured, for their support when disabled.

There is something very new and very big and very complex about these new relations of capital and labor. A new economic society has sprung up, and we must effect a new set of adjustments. We must not pit power against weakness. The employer is generally, in our day, as I have said, not an individual, but a powerful group; and yet the workingman when dealing with his employer is still, under our existing law, an individual.

Why is it that we have a labor question at all? It is for the simple and very sufficient reason that the laboring man and the employer are not intimate associates now as they used to be in time past. Most of our laws were formed in the age when employer and employees knew each other, knew each other's characters, were associates with each other, dealt with each other as man with man. That is no longer the case. You not only do not come into personal contact with the men who have the supreme command in those corporations, but it would be out of the question for you to do it. Our modern corporations employ thousands, and in some instances hundreds of thousands, of men. The only persons whom you see or deal with are local superintendents or local representatives of a vast organization, which is not like anything that the workingmen of the time in which our laws were framed knew anything about. A little group of workingmen, seeing their employer every day, dealing with him in a personal way, is one thing, and the modern body of labor engaged as employees of the huge enterprises that spread all over the country, dealing with men of whom they can form no personal conception, is another thing. A very different thing. You never saw a corporation, any more than you ever saw a government. Many a workingman to-day never saw the body of men who are conducting the industry in which he is employed. And they never saw him. What they know about him is written in ledgers and books and letters, in the correspondence of the office, in the reports of the superintendents. He is a long way off from them.

So what we have to discuss is, not wrongs which individuals intentionally do,—I do not believe there are a great many of those,—but the wrongs of a system. I want to record my protest against any discussion of this matter which would seem to indicate that there are bodies of our fellow-citizens who are trying to grind us down and do us injustice. There are some men of that sort. I don't know how they sleep o' nights, but there are men of that kind. Thank God, they are not numerous. The truth is, we are all caught in a great economic system which is heartless. The modern corporation is not engaged in business as an individual. When we deal with it, we deal with an impersonal element, an immaterial piece of society. A modern corporation is a means of co-operation in the conduct of an enterprise which is so big that no one man can conduct it, and which the resources of no one man are sufficient to finance. A company is formed; that company puts out a prospectus; the promoters expect to raise a certain fund as capital stock. Well, how are they going to raise it? They are going to raise it from the public in general, some of whom will buy their stock. The moment that begins, there is formed—what? A joint stock corporation. Men begin to pool their earnings, little piles, big piles. A certain number of men are elected by the stockholders to be directors, and these directors elect a president. This president is the head of the undertaking, and the directors are its managers.

Now, do the workingmen employed by that stock corporation deal with that president and those directors? Not at all. Does the public deal with that president and that board of directors? It does not. Can anybody bring them to account? It is next to impossible to do so. If you undertake it you will find it a game of hide and seek, with the objects of your search taking refuge now behind the tree of their individual personality, now behind that of their corporate irresponsibility.

And do our laws take note of this curious state of things? Do they even attempt to distinguish between a man's act as a corporation director and as an individual? They do not. Our laws still deal with us on the basis of the old system. The law is still living in the dead past which we have left behind. This is evident, for instance, with regard to the matter of employers' liability for workingmen's injuries. Suppose that a superintendent wants a workman to use a certain piece of machinery which it is not safe for him to use, and that the workman is injured by that piece of machinery. Some of our courts have held that the superintendent is a fellow-servant, or, as the law states it, a fellow-employee, and that, therefore, the man cannot recover damages for his injury. The superintendent who probably engaged the man is not his employer. Who is his employer? And whose negligence could conceivably come in there? The board of directors did not tell the employee to use that piece of machinery; and the president of the corporation did not tell him to use that piece of machinery. And so forth. Don't you see by that theory that a man never can get redress for negligence on the part of the employer? When I hear judges reason upon the analogy of the relationships that used to exist between workmen and their employers a generation ago, I wonder if they have not opened their eyes to the modern world. You know, we have a right to expect that judges will have their eyes open, even though the law which they administer hasn't awakened.

Yet that is but a single small detail illustrative of the difficulties we are in because we have not adjusted the law to the facts of the new order.

---

Since I entered politics, I have chiefly had men's views confided to me privately. Some of the biggest men in the United States, in the field of commerce and manufacture, are afraid of somebody, are afraid of something. They know that there is a power somewhere so organized, so subtle, so watchful, so interlocked, so complete, so pervasive, that they had better not speak above their breath when they speak in condemnation of it.

They know that America is not a place of which it can be said, as it used to be, that a man may choose his own calling and pursue it just as far as his abilities enable him to pursue it; because to-day, if he enters certain fields, there are organizations which will use means against him that will prevent his building up a business which they do not want to have built up; organizations that will see to it that the ground is cut from under him and the markets shut against him. For if he begins to sell to certain retail dealers, to any retail dealers, the monopoly will refuse to sell to those dealers, and those dealers, afraid, will not buy the new man's wares.

And this is the country which has lifted to the admiration of the world its ideals of absolutely free opportunity, where no man is supposed to be under any limitation except the limitations of his character and of his mind; where there is supposed to be no distinction of class, no distinction of blood, no distinction of social status, but where men win or lose on their merits.

I lay it very close to my own conscience as a public man whether we can any longer stand at our doors and welcome all newcomers upon those terms. American industry is not free, as once it was free; American enterprise is not free; the man with only a little capital is finding it harder to get into the field, more and more impossible to compete with the big fellow. Why? Because the laws of this country do not prevent the strong from crushing the weak. That is the reason, and because the strong have crushed the weak the strong dominate the industry and the economic life of this country. No man can deny that the lines of endeavor have more and more narrowed and stiffened; no man who knows anything about the development of industry in this country can have failed to observe that the larger kinds of credit are more and more difficult to obtain, unless you obtain them upon the terms of uniting your efforts with those who already control the industries of the country; and nobody can fail to observe that any man who tries to set himself up in competition with any process of manufacture which has been taken under the control of large combinations of capital will presently find himself either squeezed out or obliged to sell and allow himself to be absorbed.

There is a great deal that needs reconstruction in the United States. I should like to take a census of the business men,—I mean the rank and file of the business men,—as to whether they think that business conditions in this country, or rather whether the organization of business in this country, is satisfactory or not. I know what they would say if they dared. If they could vote secretly they would vote overwhelmingly that the present organization of business was meant for the big fellows and was not meant for the little fellows; that it was meant for those who are at the top and was meant to exclude those who are at the bottom; that it was meant to shut out beginners, to prevent new entries in the race, to prevent the building up of competitive enterprises that would interfere with the monopolies which the great trusts have built up.

What this country needs above everything else is a body of laws which will look after the men who are on the make rather than the men who are already made. Because the men who are already made are not going to live indefinitely, and they are not always kind enough to leave sons as able and as honest as they are.

The originative part of America, the part of America that makes new enterprises, the part into which the ambitious and gifted workingman makes his way up, the class that saves, that plans, that organizes, that presently spreads its enterprises until they have a national scope and character,—that middle class is being more and more squeezed out by the processes which we have been taught to call processes of prosperity. Its members are sharing prosperity, no doubt; but what alarms me is that they are not *originating* prosperity. No country can afford to have its prosperity originated by a small controlling class. The treasury of America does not lie in the brains of the small body of men now in control of the great enterprises that have been concentrated under the direction of a very small number of persons. The treasury of America lies in those ambitions, those energies, that cannot be restricted to a special favored class. It depends upon the inventions of unknown men, upon the originations of unknown men, upon the ambitions of unknown men. Every country is renewed out of the ranks of the unknown, not out of the ranks of those already famous and powerful and in control.

There has come over the land that un-American set of conditions which enables a small number of men who control the government to get favors from the government; by those favors to exclude their fellows from equal business opportunity; by those favors to extend a network of control that will presently dominate every industry in the country, and so make men forget the ancient time when America lay in every hamlet, when America was to be seen in every fair valley, when America displayed her great forces on the broad prairies, ran her fine fires of enterprise up over the mountainsides and down into the bowels of the earth, and eager men were everywhere captains of industry, not employees; not looking to a distant city to find out what they might do, but looking about among their neighbors, finding credit according to their character, not according to their connections, finding credit in proportion to what was known to be in them and behind them, not in proportion to the securities they held that were approved where they were not known. In order to start an enterprise now, you have to be authenticated, in a perfectly impersonal way, not according to yourself, but according to what you own that somebody else approves of your owning. You cannot begin such an enterprise as those that have made America until you are so authenticated, until you have succeeded in obtaining the good-will of large allied capitalists. Is that freedom? That is dependence, not freedom.

We used to think in the old-fashioned days when life was very simple that all that government had to do was to put on a policeman's uniform, and say, "Now don't anybody hurt anybody else." We used to say that the ideal of government was for every man to be left alone and not interfered with, except when he interfered with somebody else; and that the best government was the government that did as little governing as possible. That was the idea that obtained in Jefferson's time. But we are coming now to realize that life is so complicated that we are not dealing with the old conditions, and that the law has to step in and create new conditions under which we may live, the conditions which will make it tolerable for us to live.

Let me illustrate what I mean: It used to be true in our cities that every family occupied a separate house of its own, that every family had its own little premises, that every family was separated in its life from every other family. That is no longer the case in our great cities. Families live in tenements, they live in flats, they live on floors; they are piled layer upon layer in the great tenement houses of our crowded districts, and not only are they piled layer upon layer, but they are associated room by room, so that there is in every room, sometimes, in our congested districts, a separate family. In some foreign countries they have made much more progress than we in handling these things. In the city of Glasgow, for example (Glasgow is one of the model cities of the world), they have made up their minds that the entries and the hallways of great tenements are public streets. Therefore, the policeman goes up the stairway, and patrols the corridors; the lighting department of the city sees to it that the halls are abundantly lighted. The city does not deceive itself into supposing that that great building is a unit from which the police are to keep out and the civic authority to be excluded, but it says: "These are public highways, and light is needed in them, and control by the authority of the city."

I liken that to our great modern industrial enterprises. A corporation is very like a large tenement house; it isn't the premises of a single commercial family; it is just as much a public affair as a tenement house is a network of public highways.

When you offer the securities of a great corporation to anybody who wishes to purchase them, you must open that corporation to the inspection of everybody who wants to purchase. There must, to follow out the figure of the tenement house, be lights along the corridors, there must be police patrolling the openings, there must be inspection wherever it is known that men may be deceived with regard to the contents of the premises. If we believe that fraud lies in wait for us, we must have the means of determining whether our suspicions are well founded or not. Similarly, the treatment of labor by the great corporations is not what it was in Jefferson's time. Whenever bodies of men employ bodies of men, it ceases to be a private relationship. So that when courts hold that workingmen cannot peaceably dissuade other workingmen from taking employment, as was held in a notable case in New Jersey, they simply show that their minds and understandings are lingering in an age which has passed away. This dealing of great bodies of men with other bodies of men is a matter of public scrutiny, and should be a matter of public regulation.

Similarly, it was no business of the law in the time of Jefferson to come into my house and see how I kept house. But when my house, when my so-called private property, became a great mine, and men went along dark corridors amidst every kind of danger in order to dig out of the bowels of the earth things necessary for the industries of a whole nation, and when it came about that no individual owned these mines, that they were owned by great stock companies, then all the old analogies absolutely collapsed and it became the right of the government to go down into these mines to see whether human beings were properly treated in them or not; to see whether accidents were properly safeguarded against; to see whether modern economical methods of using these inestimable riches of the earth were followed or were not followed. If somebody puts a derrick improperly secured on top of a building or overtopping the street, then the government of the city has the right to see that that derrick is so secured that you and I can walk under it and not be afraid that the heavens are going to fall on us. Likewise, in these great beehives where in every corridor swarm men of flesh and blood, it is the privilege of the government, whether of the State or of the United States, as the case may be, to see that human life is protected, that human lungs have something to breathe.

These, again, are merely illustrations of conditions. We are in a new world, struggling under old laws. As we go inspecting our lives to-day, surveying this new scene of centralized and complex society, we shall find many more things out of joint.

---

One of the most alarming phenomena of the time,—or rather it would be alarming if the nation had not awakened to it and shown its determination to control it,—one of the most significant signs of the new social era is the degree to which government has become associated with business. I speak, for the moment, of the control over the government exercised by Big Business. Behind the whole subject, of course, is the truth that, in the new order, government and business must be associated closely. But that association is at present of a nature absolutely intolerable; the precedence is wrong, the association is upside down. Our government has been for the past few years under the control of heads of great allied corporations with special interests. It has not controlled these interests and assigned them a proper place in the whole system of business; it has submitted itself to their control. As a result, there have grown up vicious systems and schemes of governmental favoritism (the most obvious being the extravagant tariff), far-reaching in effect upon the whole fabric of life, touching to his injury every inhabitant of the land, laying unfair and impossible handicaps upon competitors, imposing taxes in every direction, stifling everywhere the free spirit of American enterprise.

Now this has come about naturally; as we go on we shall see how very naturally. It is no use denouncing anybody, or anything, except human nature. Nevertheless, it is an intolerable thing that the government of the republic should have got so far out of the hands of the people; should have been captured by interests which are special and not general. In the train of this capture follow the troops of scandals, wrongs, indecencies, with which our politics swarm.

There are cities in America of whose government we are ashamed. There are cities everywhere, in every part of the land, in which we feel that, not the interests of the public, but the interests of special privileges, of selfish men, are served; where contracts take precedence over public interest. Not only in big cities is this the case. Have you not noticed the growth of socialistic sentiment in the smaller towns? Not many months ago I stopped at a little town in Nebraska, and while my train lingered I met on the platform a very engaging young fellow dressed in overalls who introduced himself to me as the mayor of the town, and added that he was a Socialist. I said, "What does that mean? Does that mean that this town is socialistic?" "No, sir," he said; "I have not deceived myself; the vote by which I was elected was about 20 per cent. socialistic and 80 per cent. protest." It was protest against the treachery to the people of those who led both the other parties of that town.

All over the Union people are coming to feel that they have no control over the course of affairs. I live in one of the greatest States in the union, which was at one time in slavery. Until two years ago we had witnessed with increasing concern the growth in New Jersey of a spirit of almost cynical despair. Men said: "We vote; we are offered the platform we want; we elect the men who stand on that platform, and we get absolutely nothing." So they began to ask: "What is the use of voting? We know that the machines of both parties are subsidized by the same persons, and therefore it is useless to turn in either direction."

This is not confined to some of the state governments and those of some of the towns and cities. We know that something intervenes between the people of the United States and the control of their own affairs at Washington. It is not the people who have been ruling there of late.

Why are we in the presence, why are we at the threshold, of a revolution? Because we are profoundly disturbed by the influences which we see reigning in the determination of our public life and our public policy. There was a time when America was blithe with self-confidence. She boasted that she, and she alone, knew the processes of popular government; but now she sees her sky overcast; she sees that there are at work forces which she did not dream of in her hopeful youth.

Don't you know that some man with eloquent tongue, without conscience, who did not care for the nation, could put this whole country into a flame? Don't you know that this country from one end to the other believes that something is wrong? What an opportunity it would be for some man without conscience to spring up and say: "This is the way. Follow me!"—and lead in paths of destruction!

The old order changeth—changeth under our very eyes, not quietly and equably, but swiftly and with the noise and heat and tumult of reconstruction.

I suppose that all struggle for law has been conscious, that very little of it has been blind or merely instinctive. It is the fashion to say, as if with superior knowledge of affairs and of human weakness, that every age has been an age of transition, and that no age is more full of change than another; yet in very few ages of the world can the struggle for change have been so widespread, so deliberate, or upon so great a scale as in this in which we are taking part.

The transition we are witnessing is no equable transition of growth and normal alteration; no silent, unconscious unfolding of one age into another, its natural heir and successor. Society is looking itself over, in our day, from top to bottom; is making fresh and critical analysis of its very elements; is questioning its oldest practices as freely as its newest, scrutinizing every arrangement and motive of its life; and it stands ready to attempt nothing less than a radical reconstruction, which only frank and honest counsels and the forces of generous co-operation can hold back from becoming a revolution. We are in a temper to reconstruct economic society, as we were once in a temper to reconstruct political society, and political society may itself undergo a radical modification in the process. I doubt if any age was ever more conscious of its task or more unanimously desirous of radical and extended changes in its economic and political practice.

We stand in the presence of a revolution,—not a bloody revolution; America is not given to the spilling of blood,—but a silent revolution, whereby America will insist upon recovering in practice those ideals which she has always professed, upon securing a government devoted to the general interest and not to special interests.

We are upon the eve of a great reconstruction. It calls for creative statesmanship as no age has done since that great age in which we set up the government under which we live, that government which was the admiration of the world until it suffered wrongs to grow up under it which have made many of our own compatriots question the freedom of our institutions and preach revolution against them. I do not fear revolution. I have unshaken faith in the power of America to keep its self-possession. Revolution will come in peaceful guise, as it came when we put aside the crude government of the Confederation and created the great Federal Union which governs individuals, not States, and which has been these hundred and thirty years our vehicle of progress. Some radical changes we must make in our law and practice. Some reconstructions we must push forward, which a new age and new circumstances impose upon us. But we can do it all in calm and sober fashion, like statesmen and patriots.

I do not speak of these things in apprehension, because all is open and above-board. This is not a day in which great forces rally in secret. The whole stupendous program must be publicly planned and canvassed. Good temper, the wisdom that comes of sober counsel, the energy of thoughtful and unselfish men, the habit of co-operation and of compromise which has been bred in us by long years of free government, in which reason rather than passion has been made to prevail by the sheer virtue of candid and universal debate, will enable us to win through to still another great age without violence.

II

# WHAT IS PROGRESS?

In that sage and veracious chronicle, "Alice Through the Looking-Glass," it is recounted how, on a noteworthy occasion, the little heroine is seized by the Red Chess Queen, who races her off at a terrific pace. They run until both of them are out of breath; then they stop, and Alice looks around her and says, "Why, we are just where we were when we started!" "Oh, yes," says the Red Queen; "you have to run twice as fast as that to get anywhere else."

That is a parable of progress. The laws of this country have not kept up with the change of economic circumstances in this country; they have not kept up with the change of political circumstances; and therefore we are not even where we were when we started. We shall have to run, not until we are out of breath, but until we have caught up with our own conditions, before we shall be where we were when we started; when we started this great experiment which has been the hope and the beacon of the world. And we should have to run twice as fast as any rational program I have seen in order to get anywhere else.

I am, therefore, forced to be a progressive, if for no other reason, because we have not kept up with our changes of conditions, either in the economic field or in the political field. We have not kept up as well as other nations have. We have not kept our practices adjusted to the facts of the case, and until we do, and unless we do, the facts of the case will always have the better of the argument; because if you do not adjust your laws to the facts, so much the worse for the laws, not for the facts, because law trails along after the facts. Only that law is unsafe which runs ahead of the facts and beckons to it and makes it follow the will-o'-the-wisps of imaginative projects.

Business is in a situation in America which it was never in before; it is in a situation to which we have not adjusted our laws. Our laws are still meant for business done by individuals; they have not been satisfactorily adjusted to business done by great combinations, and we have got to adjust them. I do not say we may or may not; I say we must; there is no choice. If your laws do not fit your facts, the facts are not injured, the law is damaged; because the law, unless I have studied it amiss, is the expression of the facts in legal relationships. Laws have never altered the facts; laws have always necessarily expressed the facts; adjusted interests as they have arisen and have changed toward one another.

Politics in America is in a case which sadly requires attention. The system set up by our law and our usage doesn't work,—or at least it can't be depended on; it is made to work only by a most unreasonable expenditure of labor and pains. The government, which was designed for the people, has got into the hands of bosses and their employers, the special interests. An invisible empire has been set up above the forms of democracy.

There are serious things to do. Does any man doubt the great discontent in this country? Does any man doubt that there are grounds and justifications for discontent? Do we dare stand still? Within the past few months we have witnessed (along with other strange political phenomena, eloquently significant of popular uneasiness) on one side a doubling of the Socialist vote and on the other the posting on dead walls and hoardings all over the country of certain very attractive and diverting bills warning citizens that it was "better to be safe than sorry" and advising them to "let well enough alone." Apparently a good many citizens doubted whether the situation they were advised to let alone was really well enough, and concluded that they would take a chance of being sorry. To me, these counsels of do-nothingism, these counsels of sitting still for fear something would happen, these counsels addressed to the hopeful, energetic people of the United States, telling them that they are not wise enough to touch their own affairs without marring them, constitute the most extraordinary argument of fatuous ignorance I ever heard. Americans are not yet cowards. True, their self-reliance has been sapped by years of submission to the doctrine that prosperity is something that benevolent magnates provide for them with the aid of the government; their self-reliance has been weakened, but not so utterly destroyed that you can twit them about it. The American people are not naturally stand-patters. Progress is the word that charms their ears and stirs their hearts.

There are, of course, Americans who have not yet heard that anything is going on. The circus might come to town, have the big parade and go, without their catching a sight of the camels or a note of the calliope. There are people, even Americans, who never move themselves or know that anything else is moving.

A friend of mine who had heard of the Florida "cracker," as they call a certain ne'er-do-weel portion of the population down there, when passing through the State in a train, asked some one to point out a "cracker" to him. The man asked replied, "Well, if you see something off in the woods that looks brown, like a stump, you will know it is either a stump or a cracker; if it moves, it is a stump."

Now, movement has no virtue in itself. Change is not worth while for its own sake. I am not one of those who love variety for its own sake. If a thing is good to-day, I should like to have it stay that way to-morrow. Most of our calculations in life are dependent upon things staying the way they are. For example, if, when you got up this morning, you had forgotten how to dress, if you had forgotten all about those ordinary things which you do almost automatically, which you can almost do half awake, you would have to find out what you did yesterday. I am told by the psychologists that if I did not remember who I was yesterday, I should not know who I am to-day, and that, therefore, my very identity depends upon my being able to tally to-day with yesterday. If they do not tally, then I am confused; I do not know who I am, and I have to go around and ask somebody to tell me my name and where I came from.

I am not one of those who wish to break connection with the past; I am not one of those who wish to change for the mere sake of variety. The only men who do that are the men who want to forget something, the men who filled yesterday with something they would rather not recollect to-day, and so go about seeking diversion, seeking abstraction in something that will blot out recollection, or seeking to put something into them which will blot out all recollection. Change is not worth while unless it is improvement. If I move out of my present house because I do not like it, then I have got to choose a better house, or build a better house, to justify the change.

It would seem a waste of time to point out that ancient distinction,—between mere change and improvement. Yet there is a class of mind that is prone to confuse them. We have had political leaders whose conception of greatness was to be forever frantically doing something,—it mattered little what; restless, vociferous men, without sense of the energy of concentration, knowing only the energy of succession. Now, life does not consist of eternally running to a fire. There is no virtue in going anywhere unless you will gain something by being there. The direction is just as important as the impetus of motion.

All progress depends on how fast you are going, and where you are going, and I fear there has been too much of this thing of knowing neither how fast we were going or where we were going. I have my private belief that we have been doing most of our progressiveness after the fashion of those things that in my boyhood days we called "treadmills,"—a treadmill being a moving platform, with cleats on it, on which some poor devil of a mule was forced to walk forever without getting anywhere. Elephants and even other animals have been known to turn treadmills, making a good deal of noise, and causing certain wheels to go round, and I daresay grinding out some sort of product for somebody, but without achieving much progress. Lately, in an effort to persuade the elephant to move, really, his friends tried dynamite. It moved,—in separate and scattered parts, but it moved.

A cynical but witty Englishman said, in a book, not long ago, that it was a mistake to say of a conspicuously successful man, eminent in his line of business, that you could not bribe a man like that, because, he said, the point about such men is that they have been bribed—not in the ordinary meaning of that word, not in any gross, corrupt sense, but they have achieved their great success by means of the existing order of things and therefore they have been put under bonds to see that that existing order of things is not changed; they are bribed to maintain the *status quo*.

It was for that reason that I used to say, when I had to do with the administration of an educational institution, that I should like to make the young gentlemen of the rising generation as unlike their fathers as possible. Not because their fathers lacked character or intelligence or knowledge or patriotism, but because their fathers, by reason of their advancing years and their established position in society, had lost touch with the processes of life; they had forgotten what it was to begin; they had forgotten what it was to rise; they had forgotten what it was to be dominated by the circumstances of their life on their way up from the bottom to the top, and, therefore, they were out of sympathy with the creative, formative and progressive forces of society.

Progress! Did you ever reflect that that word is almost a new one? No word comes more often or more naturally to the lips of modern man, as if the thing it stands for were almost synonymous with life itself, and yet men through many thousand years never talked or thought of progress. They thought in the other direction. Their stories of heroisms and glory were tales of the past. The ancestor wore the heavier armor and carried the larger spear. "There were giants in those days." Now all that has altered. We think of the future, not the past, as the more glorious time in comparison with which the present is nothing. Progress, development,—those are modern words. The modern idea is to leave the past and press onward to something new.

But what is progress going to do with the past, and with the present? How is it going to treat them? With ignominy, or respect? Should it break with them altogether, or rise out of them, with its roots still deep in the older time? What attitude shall progressives take toward the existing order, toward those institutions of conservatism, the Constitution, the laws, and the courts?

Are those thoughtful men who fear that we are now about to disturb the ancient foundations of our institutions justified in their fear? If they are, we ought to go very slowly about the processes of change. If it is indeed true that we have grown tired of the institutions which we have so carefully and sedulously built up, then we ought to go very slowly and very carefully about the very dangerous task of altering them. We ought, therefore, to ask ourselves, first of all, whether thought in this country is tending to do anything by which we shall retrace our steps, or by which we shall change the whole direction of our development?

I believe, for one, that you cannot tear up ancient rootages and safely plant the tree of liberty in soil which is not native to it. I believe that the ancient traditions of a people are its ballast; you cannot make a *tabula rasa* upon which to write a political program. You cannot take a new sheet of paper and determine what your life shall be to-morrow. You must knit the new into the old. You cannot put a new patch on an old garment without ruining it; it must be not a patch, but something woven into the old fabric, of practically the same pattern, of the same texture and intention. If I did not believe that to be progressive was to preserve the essentials of our institutions, I for one could not be a progressive.

---

One of the chief benefits I used to derive from being president of a university was that I had the pleasure of entertaining thoughtful men from all over the world. I cannot tell you how much has dropped into my granary by their presence. I had been casting around in my mind for something by which to draw several parts of my political thought together when it was my good fortune to entertain a very interesting Scotsman who had been devoting himself to the philosophical thought of the seventeenth century. His talk was so engaging that it was delightful to hear him speak of anything, and presently there came out of the unexpected region of his thought the thing I had been waiting for. He called my attention to the fact that in every generation all sorts of speculation and thinking tend to fall under the formula of the dominant thought of the age. For example, after the Newtonian Theory of the universe had been developed, almost all thinking tended to express itself in the analogies of the Newtonian Theory, and since the Darwinian Theory has reigned amongst us, everybody is likely to express whatever he wishes to expound in terms of development and accommodation to environment.

Now, it came to me, as this interesting man talked, that the Constitution of the United States had been made under the dominion of the Newtonian Theory. You have only to read the papers of *The Federalist* to see that fact written on every page. They speak of the "checks and balances" of the Constitution, and use to express their idea the simile of the organization of the universe, and particularly of the solar system,—how by the attraction of gravitation the various parts are held in their orbits; and then they proceed to represent Congress, the Judiciary, and the President as a sort of imitation of the solar system.

They were only following the English Whigs, who gave Great Britain its modern constitution. Not that those Englishmen analyzed the matter, or had any theory about it; Englishmen care little for theories. It was a Frenchman, Montesquieu, who pointed out to them how faithfully they had copied Newton's description of the mechanism of the heavens.

The makers of our Federal Constitution read Montesquieu with true scientific enthusiasm. They were scientists in their way,—the best way of their age,—those fathers of the nation. Jefferson wrote of "the laws of Nature,"—and then by way of afterthought,—"and of Nature's God." And they constructed a government as they would have constructed an orrery,—to display the laws of nature. Politics in their thought was a variety of mechanics. The Constitution was founded on the law of gravitation. The government was to exist and move by virtue of the efficacy of "checks and balances."

The trouble with the theory is that government is not a machine, but a living thing. It falls, not under the theory of the universe, but under the theory of organic life. It is accountable to Darwin, not to Newton. It is modified by its environment, necessitated by its tasks, shaped to its functions by the sheer pressure of life. No living thing can have its organs offset against each other, as checks, and live. On the contrary, its life is dependent upon their quick co-operation, their ready response to the commands of instinct or intelligence, their amicable community of purpose. Government is not a body of blind forces; it is a body of men, with highly differentiated functions, no doubt, in our modern day, of specialization, with a common task and purpose. Their co-operation is indispensable, their warfare fatal. There can be no successful government without the intimate, instinctive co-ordination of the organs of life and action. This is not theory, but fact, and displays its force as fact, whatever theories may be thrown across its track. Living political constitutions must be Darwinian in structure and in practice. Society is a living organism and must obey the laws of life, not of mechanics; it must develop.

All that progressives ask or desire is permission—in an era when "development," "evolution," is the scientific word—to interpret the Constitution according to the Darwinian principle; all they ask is recognition of the fact that a nation is a living thing and not a machine.

Some citizens of this country have never got beyond the Declaration of Independence, signed in Philadelphia, July 4th, 1776. Their bosoms swell against George III, but they have no consciousness of the war for freedom that is going on to-day.

The Declaration of Independence did not mention the questions of our day. It is of no consequence to us unless we can translate its general terms into examples of the present day and substitute them in some vital way for the examples it itself gives, so concrete, so intimately involved in the circumstances of the day in which it was conceived and written. It is an eminently practical document, meant for the use of practical men; not a thesis for philosophers, but a whip for tyrants; not a theory of government, but a program of action. Unless we can translate it into the questions of our own day, we are not worthy of it, we are not the sons of the sires who acted in response to its challenge.

What form does the contest between tyranny and freedom take to-day? What is the special form of tyranny we now fight? How does it endanger the rights of the people, and what do we mean to do in order to make our contest against it effectual? What are to be the items of our new declaration of independence?

By tyranny, as we now fight it, we mean control of the law, of legislation and adjudication, by organizations which do not represent the people, by means which are private and selfish. We mean, specifically, the conduct of our affairs and the shaping of our legislation in the interest of special bodies of capital and those who organize their use. We mean the alliance, for this purpose, of political machines with selfish business. We mean the exploitation of the people by legal and political means. We have seen many of our governments under these influences cease to be representative governments, cease to be governments representative of the people, and become governments representative of special interests, controlled by machines, which in their turn are not controlled by the people.

Sometimes, when I think of the growth of our economic system, it seems to me as if, leaving our law just about where it was before any of the modern inventions or developments took place, we had simply at haphazard extended the family residence, added an office here and a workroom there, and a new set of sleeping rooms there, built up higher on our foundations, and put out little lean-tos on the side, until we have a structure that has no character whatever. Now, the problem is to continue to live in the house and yet change it.

Well, we are architects in our time, and our architects are also engineers. We don't have to stop using a railroad terminal because a new station is being built. We don't have to stop any of the processes of our lives because we are rearranging the structures in which we conduct those processes. What we have to undertake is to systematize the foundations of the house, then to thread all the old parts of the structure with the steel which will be laced together in modern fashion, accommodated to all the modern knowledge of structural strength and elasticity, and then slowly change the partitions, relay the walls, let in the light through new apertures, improve the ventilation; until finally, a generation or two from now, the scaffolding will be taken away, and there will be the family in a great building whose noble architecture will at last be disclosed, where men can live as a single community, co-operative as in a perfected, co-ordinated beehive, not afraid of any storm of nature, not afraid of any artificial storm, any imitation of thunder and lightning, knowing that the foundations go down to the bedrock of principle, and knowing that whenever they please they can change that plan again and accommodate it as they please to the altering necessities of their lives.

But there are a great many men who don't like the idea. Some wit recently said, in view of the fact that most of our American architects are trained in a certain *École* in Paris, that all American architecture in recent years was either bizarre or "Beaux Arts." I think that our economic architecture is decidedly bizarre; and I am afraid that there is a good deal to learn about matters other than architecture from the same source from which our architects have learned a great many things. I don't mean the School of Fine Arts at Paris, but the experience of France; for from the other side of the water men can now hold up against us the reproach that we have not adjusted our lives to modern conditions to the same extent that they have adjusted theirs. I was very much interested in some of the reasons given by our friends across the Canadian border for being very shy about the reciprocity arrangements. They said: "We are not sure whither these arrangements will lead, and we don't care to associate too closely with the economic conditions of the United States until those conditions are as modern as ours." And when I resented it, and asked for particulars, I had, in regard to many matters, to retire from the debate. Because I found that they had adjusted their regulations of economic development to conditions we had not yet found a way to meet in the United States.

Well, we have started now at all events. The procession is under way. The stand-patter doesn't know there is a procession. He is asleep in the back part of his house. He doesn't know that the road is resounding with the tramp of men going to the front. And when he wakes up, the country will be empty. He will be deserted, and he will wonder what has happened. Nothing has happened. The world has been going on. The world has a habit of going on. The world has a habit of leaving those behind who won't go with it. The world has always neglected stand-patters. And, therefore, the stand-patter does not excite my indignation; he excites my sympathy. He is going to be so lonely before it is all over. And we are good fellows, we are good company; why doesn't he come along? We are not going to do him any harm. We are going to show him a good time. We are going to climb the slow road until it reaches some upland where the air is fresher, where the whole talk of mere politicians is stilled, where men can look in each other's faces and see that there is nothing to conceal, that all they have to talk about they are willing to talk about in the open and talk about with each other; and whence, looking back over the road, we shall see at last that we have fulfilled our promise to mankind. We had said to all the world, "America was created to break every kind of monopoly, and to set men free, upon a footing of equality, upon a footing of opportunity, to match their brains and their energies." and now we have proved that we meant it.

# III

# FREEMEN NEED NO GUARDIANS

There are two theories of government that have been contending with each other ever since government began. One of them is the theory which in America is associated with the name of a very great man, Alexander Hamilton. A great man, but, in my judgment, not a great American. He did not think in terms of American life. Hamilton believed that the only people who could understand government, and therefore the only people who were qualified to conduct it, were the men who had the biggest financial stake in the commercial and industrial enterprises of the country.

That theory, though few have now the hardihood to profess it openly, has been the working theory upon which our government has lately been conducted. It is astonishing how persistent it is. It is amazing how quickly the political party which had Lincoln for its first leader,—Lincoln, who not only denied, but in his own person so completely disproved the aristocratic theory,—it is amazing how quickly that party, founded on faith in the people, forgot the precepts of Lincoln and fell under the delusion that the "masses" needed the guardianship of "men of affairs."

For indeed, if you stop to think about it, nothing could be a greater departure from original Americanism, from faith in the ability of a confident, resourceful, and independent people, than the discouraging doctrine that somebody has got to provide prosperity for the rest of us. And yet that is exactly the doctrine on which the government of the United States has been conducted lately. Who have been consulted when important measures of government, like tariff acts, and currency acts, and railroad acts, were under consideration? The people whom the tariff chiefly affects, the people for whom the currency is supposed to exist, the people who pay the duties and ride on the railroads? Oh, no! What do they know about such matters! The gentlemen whose ideas have been sought are the big manufacturers, the bankers, and the heads of the great railroad combinations. The masters of the government of the United States are the combined capitalists and manufacturers of the United States. It is written over every intimate page of the records of Congress, it is written all through the history of conferences at the White House, that the suggestions of economic policy in this country have come from one source, not from many sources. The benevolent guardians, the kind-hearted trustees who have taken the troubles of government off our hands, have become so conspicuous that almost anybody can write out a list of them. They have become so conspicuous that their names are mentioned upon almost every political platform. The men who have undertaken the interesting job of taking care of us do not force us to requite them with anonymously directed gratitude. We know them by name.

Suppose you go to Washington and try to get at your government. You will always find that while you are politely listened to, the men really consulted are the men who have the biggest stake,—the big bankers, the big manufacturers, the big masters of commerce, the heads of railroad corporations and of steamship corporations. I have no objection to these men being consulted, because they also, though they do not themselves seem to admit it, are part of the people of the United States. But I do very seriously object to these gentlemen being *chiefly* consulted, and particularly to their being exclusively consulted, for, if the government of the United States is to do the right thing by the people of the United States, it has got to do it directly and not through the intermediation of these gentlemen. Every time it has come to a critical question these gentlemen have been yielded to, and their demands have been treated as the demands that should be followed as a matter of course.

The government of the United States at present is a foster-child of the special interests. It is not allowed to have a will of its own. It is told at every move: "Don't do that; you will interfere with our prosperity." And when we ask, "Where is our prosperity lodged?" a certain group of gentlemen say, "With us." The government of the United States in recent years has not been administered by the common people of the United States. You know just as well as I do,—it is not an indictment against anybody, it is a mere statement of the facts,—that the people have stood outside and looked on at their own government and that all they have had to determine in past years has been which crowd they would look on at; whether they would look on at this little group or that little group who had managed to get the control of affairs in its hands. Have you ever heard, for example, of any hearing before any great committee of the Congress in which the people of the country as a whole were represented, except it may be by the Congressmen themselves? The men who appear at those meetings in order to argue for or against a schedule in the tariff, for this measure or against that measure, are men who represent special interests. They may represent them very honestly, they may intend no wrong to their fellow-citizens, but they are speaking from the point of view always of a small portion of the population. I have sometimes wondered why men, particularly men of means, men who didn't have to work for their living, shouldn't constitute themselves attorneys for the people, and every time a hearing is held before a committee of Congress should not go and ask: "Gentlemen, in considering these things suppose you consider the whole country? Suppose you consider the citizens of the United States?"

I don't want a smug lot of experts to sit down behind closed doors in Washington and play Providence to me. There is a Providence to which I am perfectly willing to submit. But as for other men setting up as Providence over myself, I seriously object. I have never met a political savior in the flesh, and I never expect to meet one. I am reminded of Gillet Burgess' verses:

> I never saw a purple cow,
> I never hope to see one,
> But this I'll tell you anyhow,
> I'd rather see than be one.

That is the way I feel about this saving of my fellow-countrymen. I'd rather see a savior of the United States than set up to be one; because I have found out, I have actually found out, that men I consult with know more than I do, —especially if I consult with enough of them. I never came out of a committee meeting or a conference without seeing more of the question that was under discussion than I had seen when I went in. And that to my mind is an image of government. I am not willing to be under the patronage of the trusts, no matter how providential a government presides over the process of their control of my life.

I am one of those who absolutely reject the trustee theory, the guardianship theory. I have never found a man who knew how to take care of me, and, reasoning from that point out, I conjecture that there isn't any man who knows how to take care of all the people of the United States. I suspect that the people of the United States understand their own interests better than any group of men in the confines of the country understand them. The men who are sweating blood to get their foothold in the world of endeavor understand the conditions of business in the United States very much better than the men who have arrived and are at the top. They know what the thing is that they are struggling against. They know how difficult it is to start a new enterprise. They know how far they have to search for credit that will put them upon an even footing with the men who have already built up industry in this country. They know that somewhere, by somebody, the development of industry is being controlled.

I do not say this with the slightest desire to create any prejudice against wealth; on the contrary, I should be ashamed of myself if I excited class feeling of any kind. But I do mean to suggest this: That the wealth of the country has, in recent years, come from particular sources; it has come from those sources which have built up monopoly. Its point of view is a special point of view. It is the point of view of those men who do not wish that the people should determine their own affairs, because they do not believe that the people's judgment is sound. They want to be commissioned to take care of the United States and of the people of the United States, because they believe that they, better than anybody else, understand the interests of the United States. I do not challenge their character; I challenge their point of view. We cannot afford to be governed as we have been governed in the last generation, by men who occupy so narrow, so prejudiced, so limited a point of view.

The government of our country cannot be lodged in any special class. The policy of a great nation cannot be tied up with any particular set of interests. I want to say, again and again, that my arguments do not touch the character of the men to whom I am opposed. I believe that the very wealthy men who have got their money by certain kinds of corporate enterprise have closed in their horizon, and that they do not see and do not understand the rank and file of the people. It is for that reason that I want to break up the little coterie that has determined what the government of the nation should do. The list of the men who used to determine what New Jersey should and should not do did not exceed half a dozen, and they were always the same men. These very men now are, some of them, frank enough to admit that New Jersey has finer energy in her because more men are consulted and the whole field of action is widened and liberalized. We have got to relieve our government from the domination of special classes, not because these special classes are bad, necessarily, but because no special class can understand the interests of a great community.

I believe, as I believe in nothing else, in the average integrity and the average intelligence of the American people, and I do not believe that the intelligence of America can be put into commission anywhere. I do not believe that there is any group of men of any kind to whom we can afford to give that kind of trusteeship.

I will not live under trustees if I can help it. No group of men less than the majority has a right to tell me how I have got to live in America. I will submit to the majority, because I have been trained to do it,—though I may sometimes have my private opinion even of the majority. I do not care how wise, how patriotic, the trustees may be, I have never heard of any group of men in whose hands I am willing to lodge the liberties of America in trust.

If any part of our people want to be wards, if they want to have guardians put over them, if they want to be taken care of, if they want to be children, patronized by the government, why, I am sorry, because it will sap the manhood of America. But I don't believe they do. I believe they want to stand on the firm foundation of law and right and take care of themselves. I, for my part, don't want to belong to a nation, I believe that I do not belong to a nation, that needs to be taken care of by guardians. I want to belong to a nation, and I am proud that I do belong to a nation, that knows how to take care of itself. If I thought that the American people were reckless, were ignorant, were vindictive, I might shrink from putting the government into their hands. But the beauty of democracy is that when you are reckless you destroy your own established conditions of life; when you are vindictive, you wreak vengeance upon yourself; the whole stability of a democratic polity rests upon the fact that every interest is every man's interest.

The theory that the men of biggest affairs, whose field of operation is the widest, are the proper men to advise the government is, I am willing to admit, rather a plausible theory. If my business covers the United States not only, but covers the world, it is to be presumed that I have a pretty wide scope in my vision of business. But the flaw is that it is my own business that I have a vision of, and not the business of the men who lie outside of the scope of the plans I have made for a profit out of the particular transactions I am connected with. And you can't, by putting together a large number of men who understand their own business, no matter how large it is, make up a body of men who will understand the business of the nation as contrasted with their own interest.

In a former generation, half a century ago, there were a great many men associated with the government whose patriotism we are not privileged to deny nor to question, who intended to serve the people, but had become so saturated with the point of view of a governing class that it was impossible for them to see America as the people of America themselves saw it. Then there arose that interesting figure, the immortal figure of the great Lincoln, who stood up declaring that the politicians, the men who had governed this country, did not see from the point of view of the people. When I think of that tall, gaunt figure rising in Illinois, I have a picture of a man free, unentangled, unassociated with the governing influences of the country, ready to see things with an open eye, to see them steadily, to see them whole, to see them as the men he rubbed shoulders with and associated with saw them. What the country needed in 1860 was a leader who understood and represented the thought of the whole people, as contrasted with that of a class which imagined itself the guardian of the country's welfare.

Now, likewise, the trouble with our present political condition is that we need some man who has not been associated with the governing classes and the governing influences of this country to stand up and speak for us; we need to hear a voice from the outside calling upon the American people to assert again their rights and prerogatives in the possession of their own government.

My thought about both Mr. Taft and Mr. Roosevelt is that of entire respect, but these gentlemen have been so intimately associated with the powers that have been determining the policy of this government for almost a generation, that they cannot look at the affairs of the country with the view of a new age and of a changed set of circumstances. They sympathize with the people; their hearts no doubt go out to the great masses of unknown men in this country; but their thought is in close, habitual association with those who have framed the policies of the country during all our lifetime. Those men have framed the protective tariff, have developed the trusts, have co-ordinated and ordered all the great economic forces of this country in such fashion that nothing but an outside force breaking in can disturb their domination and control. It is with this in mind, I believe, that the country can say to these gentlemen: "We do not deny your integrity; we do not deny your purity of purpose; but the thought of the people of the United States has not yet penetrated to your consciousness. You are willing to act for the people, but you are not willing to act *through* the people. Now we propose to act for ourselves."

---

I sometimes think that the men who are now governing us are unconscious of the chains in which they are held. I do not believe that men such as we know, among our public men at least—most of them—have deliberately put us into leading strings to the special interests. The special interests have grown up. They have grown up by processes which at last, happily, we are beginning to understand. And, having grown up, having occupied the seats of greatest advantage nearest the ear of those who are conducting government, having contributed the money which was necessary to the elections, and therefore having been kindly thought of after elections, there has closed around the government of the United States a very interesting, a very able, a very aggressive coterie of gentlemen who are most definite and explicit in their ideas as to what they want.

They don't have to consult us as to what they want. They don't have to resort to anybody. They know their plans, and therefore they know what will be convenient for them. It may be that they have really thought what they have said they thought; it may be that they know so little of the history of economic development and of the interests of the United States as to believe that their leadership is indispensable for our prosperity and development. I don't have to prove that they believe that, because they themselves admit it. I have heard them admit it on many occasions.

I want to say to you very frankly that I do not feel vindictive about it. Some of the men who have exercised this control are excellent fellows; they really believe that the prosperity of the country depends upon them. They really believe that if the leadership of economic development in this country dropped from their hands, the rest of us are too muddle-headed to undertake the task. They not only comprehend the power of the United States within their grasp, but they comprehend it within their imagination. They are honest men, they have just as much right to express their views as I have to express mine or you to express yours, but it is just about time that we examined their views for ourselves and determined their validity.

As a matter of fact, their thought does not cover the processes of their own undertakings. As a university president, I learned that the men who dominate our manufacturing processes could not conduct their business for twenty-four hours without the assistance of the experts with whom the universities were supplying them. Modern industry depends upon technical knowledge; and all that these gentlemen did was to manage the external features of great combinations and their financial operation, which had very little to do with the intimate skill with which the enterprises were conducted. I know men not catalogued in the public prints, men not spoken of in public discussion, who are the very bone and sinew of the industry of the United States.

Do our masters of industry speak in the spirit and interest even of those whom they employ? When men ask me what I think about the labor question and laboring men, I feel that I am being asked what I know about the vast majority of the people, and I feel as if I were being asked to separate myself, as belonging to a particular class, from that great body of my fellow-citizens who sustain and conduct the enterprises of the country. Until we get away from that point of view it will be impossible to have a free government.

I have listened to some very honest and eloquent orators whose sentiments were noteworthy for this: that when they spoke of the people, they were not thinking of themselves; they were thinking of somebody whom they were commissioned to take care of. They were always planning to do things *for* the American people, and I have seen them visibly shiver when it was suggested that they arrange to have something done by the people for themselves. They said, "What do they know about it?" I always feel like replying, "What do *you* know about it? You know your own interest, but who has told you our interests, and what do you know about them?" For the business of every leader of government is to hear what the nation is saying and to know what the nation is enduring. It is not his business to judge *for* the nation, but to judge *through* the nation as its spokesman and voice. I do not believe that this country could have safely allowed a continuation of the policy of the men who have viewed affairs in any other light.

The hypothesis under which we have been ruled is that of government through a board of trustees, through a selected number of the big business men of the country who know a lot that the rest of us do not know, and who take it for granted that our ignorance would wreck the prosperity of the country. The idea of the Presidents we have recently had has been that they were Presidents of a National Board of Trustees. That is not my idea. I have been president of one board of trustees, and I do not care to have another on my hands. I want to be President of the people of the United States. There was many a time when I was president of the board of trustees of a university when the undergraduates knew more than the trustees did; and it has been in my thought ever since that if I could have dealt directly with the people who constituted Princeton University I could have carried it forward much faster than I could dealing with a board of trustees.

Mark you, I am not saying that these leaders knew that they were doing us an evil, or that they intended to do us an evil. For my part, I am very much more afraid of the man who does a bad thing and does not know it is bad than of the man who does a bad thing and knows it is bad; because I think that in public affairs stupidity is more dangerous than knavery, because harder to fight and dislodge. If a man does not know enough to know what the consequences are going to be to the country, then he cannot govern the country in a way that is for its benefit. These gentlemen, whatever may have been their intentions, linked the government up with the men who control the finances. They may have done it innocently, or they may have done it corruptly, without affecting my argument at all. And they themselves cannot escape from that alliance.

Here, for example, is the old question of campaign funds: If I take a hundred thousand dollars from a group of men representing a particular interest that has a big stake in a certain schedule of the tariff, I take it with the knowledge that those gentlemen will expect me not to forget their interest in that schedule, and that they will take it as a point of implicit honor that I should see to it that they are not damaged by too great a change in that schedule. Therefore, if I take their money, I am bound to them by a tacit implication of honor. Perhaps there is no ground for objection to this situation so long as the function of government is conceived to be to look after the trustees of prosperity, who in turn will look after the people; but on any other theory than that of trusteeship no interested campaign contributions can be tolerated for a moment,—save those of the millions of citizens who thus support the doctrines they believe and the men whom they recognized as their spokesmen.

I tell you the men I am interested in are the men who, under the conditions we have had, never had their voices heard, who never got a line in the newspapers, who never got a moment on the platform, who never had access to the ears of Governors or Presidents or of anybody who was responsible for the conduct of public affairs, but who went silently and patiently to their work every day carrying the burden of the world. How are they to be understood by the masters of finance, if only the masters of finance are consulted?

---

That is what I mean when I say, "Bring the government back to the people." I do not mean anything demagogic; I do not mean to talk as if we wanted a great mass of men to rush in and destroy something. That is not the idea. I want the people to come in and take possession of their own premises; for I hold that the government belongs to the people, and that they have a right to that intimate access to it which will determine every turn of its policy.

America is never going to submit to guardianship. America is never going to choose thralldom instead of freedom. Look what there is to decide! There is the tariff question. Can the tariff question be decided in favor of the people, so long as the monopolies are the chief counselors at Washington? There is the currency question. Are we going to settle the currency question so long as the government listens only to the counsel of those who command the banking situation?

Then there is the question of conservation. What is our fear about conservation? The hands that are being stretched out to monopolize our forests, to prevent or pre-empt the use of our great power-producing streams, the hands that are being stretched into the bowels of the earth to take possession of the great riches that lie hidden in Alaska and elsewhere in the incomparable domain of the United States, are the hands of monopoly. Are these men to continue to stand at the elbow of government and tell us how we are to save ourselves,—from themselves? You can not settle the question of conservation while monopoly is close to the ears of those who govern. And the question of conservation is a great deal bigger than the question of saving our forests and our mineral resources and our waters; it is as big as the life and happiness and strength and elasticity and hope of our people.

There are tasks awaiting the government of the United States which it cannot perform until every pulse of that government beats in unison with the needs and the desires of the whole body of the American people. Shall we not give the people access of sympathy, access of authority, to the instrumentalities which are to be indispensable to their lives?

---

**IV**

# LIFE COMES FROM THE SOIL

When I look back on the processes of history, when I survey the genesis of America, I see this written over every page: that the nations are renewed from the bottom, not from the top; that the genius which springs up from the ranks of unknown men is the genius which renews the youth and energy of the people. Everything I know about history, every bit of experience and observation that has contributed to my thought, has confirmed me in the conviction that the real wisdom of human life is compounded out of the experiences of ordinary men. The utility, the vitality, the fruitage of life does not come from the top to the bottom; it comes, like the natural growth of a great tree, from the soil, up through the trunk into the branches to the foliage and the fruit. The great struggling unknown masses of the men who are at the base of everything are the dynamic force that is lifting the levels of society. A nation is as great, and only as great, as her rank and file.

So the first and chief need of this nation of ours to-day is to include in the partnership of government all those great bodies of unnamed men who are going to produce our future leaders and renew the future energies of America. And as I confess that, as I confess my belief in the common man, I know what I am saying. The man who is swimming against the stream knows the strength of it. The man who is in the mêlée knows what blows are being struck and what blood is being drawn. The man who is on the make is the judge of what is happening in America, not the man who has made good; not the man who has emerged from the flood; not the man who is standing on the bank looking on, but the man who is struggling for his life and for the lives of those who are dearer to him than himself. That is the man whose judgment will tell you what is going on in America; that is the man by whose judgment I, for one, wish to be guided.

We have had the wrong jury; we have had the wrong group,—no, I will not say the wrong group, but too small a group,—in control of the policies of the United States. The average man has not been consulted, and his heart had begun to sink for fear he never would be consulted again. Therefore, we have got to organize a government whose sympathies will be open to the whole body of the people of the United States, a government which will consult as large a proportion of the people of the United States as possible before it acts. Because the great problem of government is to know what the average man is experiencing and is thinking about. Most of us are average men; very few of us rise, except by fortunate accident, above the general level of the community about us; and therefore the man who thinks common thoughts, the man who has had common experiences, is almost always the man who interprets America aright. Isn't that the reason that we are proud of such stories as the story of Abraham Lincoln,—a man who rose out of the ranks and interpreted America better than any man had interpreted it who had risen out of the privileged classes or the educated classes of America?

The hope of the United States in the present and in the future is the same that it has always been: it is the hope and confidence that out of unknown homes will come men who will constitute themselves the masters of industry and of politics. The average hopefulness, the average welfare, the average enterprise, the average initiative, of the United States are the only things that make it rich. We are not rich because a few gentlemen direct our industry; we are rich because of our own intelligence and our own industry. America does not consist of men who get their names into the newspapers; America does not consist politically of the men who set themselves up to be political leaders; she does not consist of the men who do most of her talking,—they are important only so far as they speak for that great voiceless multitude of men who constitute the great body and the saving force of the nation. Nobody who cannot speak the common thought, who does not move by the common impulse, is the man to speak for America, or for any of her future purposes. Only he is fit to speak who knows the thoughts of the great body of citizens, the men who go about their business every day, the men who toil from morning till night, the men who go home tired in the evenings, the men who are carrying on the things we are so proud of.

You know how it thrills our blood sometimes to think how all the nations of the earth wait to see what America is going to do with her power, her physical power, her enormous resources, her enormous wealth. The nations hold their breath to see what this young country will do with her young unspoiled strength; we cannot help but be proud that we are strong. But what has made us strong? The toil of millions of men, the toil of men who do not boast, who are inconspicuous, but who live their lives humbly from day to day; it is the great body of toilers that constitutes the might of America. It is one of the glories of our land that nobody is able to predict from what family, from what region, from what race, even, the leaders of the country are going to come. The great leaders of this country have not come very often from the established, "successful" families.

I remember speaking at a school not long ago where I understood that almost all the young men were the sons of very rich people, and I told them I looked upon them with a great deal of pity, because, I said: "Most of you fellows are doomed to obscurity. You will not do anything. You will never try to do anything, and with all the great tasks of the country waiting to be done, probably you are the very men who will decline to do them. Some man who has been 'up against it,' some man who has come out of the crowd, somebody who has had the whip of necessity laid on his back, will emerge out of the crowd, will show that he understands the crowd, understands the interests of the nation, united and not separated, and will stand up and lead us."

If I may speak of my own experience, I have found audiences made up of the "common people" quicker to take a point, quicker to understand an argument, quicker to discern a tendency and to comprehend a principle, than many a college class that I have lectured to,—not because the college class lacked the intelligence, but because college boys are not in contact with the realities of life, while "common" citizens are in contact with the actual life of day by day; you do not have to explain to them what touches them to the quick.

There is one illustration of the value of the constant renewal of society from the bottom that has always interested me profoundly. The only reason why government did not suffer dry rot in the Middle Ages under the aristocratic system which then prevailed was that so many of the men who were efficient instruments of government were drawn from the church,—from that great religious body which was then the only church, that body which we now distinguish from other religious bodies as the Roman Catholic Church. The Roman Catholic Church was then, as it is now, a great democracy. There was no peasant so humble that he might not become a priest, and no priest so obscure that he might not become Pope of Christendom; and every chancellery in Europe, every court in Europe, was ruled by these learned, trained and accomplished men,—the priesthood of that great and dominant body. What kept government alive in the Middle Ages was this constant rise of the sap from the bottom, from the rank and file of the great body of the people through the open channels of the priesthood. That, it seems to me, is one of the most interesting and convincing illustrations that could possibly be adduced of the thing that I am talking about.

The only way that government is kept pure is by keeping these channels open, so that nobody may deem himself so humble as not to constitute a part of the body politic, so that there will constantly be coming new blood into the veins of the body politic; so that no man is so obscure that he may not break the crust of any class he may belong to, may not spring up to higher levels and be counted among the leaders of the state. Anything that depresses, anything that makes the organization greater than the man, anything that blocks, discourages, dismays the humble man, is against all the principles of progress. When I see alliances formed, as they are now being formed, by successful men of business with successful organizers of politics, I know that something has been done that checks the vitality and progress of society. Such an alliance, made at the top, is an alliance made to depress the levels, to hold them where they are, if not to sink them; and, therefore, it is the constant business of good politics to break up such partnerships, to re-establish and reopen the connections between the great body of the people and the offices of government.

To-day, when our government has so far passed into the hands of special interests; to-day, when the doctrine is implicitly avowed that only select classes have the equipment necessary for carrying on government; to-day, when so many conscientious citizens, smitten with the scene of social wrong and suffering, have fallen victims to the fallacy that benevolent government can be meted out to the people by kind-hearted trustees of prosperity and guardians of the welfare of dutiful employees,—to-day, supremely, does it behoove this nation to remember that a people shall be saved by the power that sleeps in its own deep bosom, or by none; shall be renewed in hope, in conscience, in strength, by waters welling up from its own sweet, perennial springs. Not from above; not by patronage of its aristocrats. The flower does not bear the root, but the root the flower. Everything that blooms in beauty in the air of heaven draws its fairness, its vigor, from its roots. Nothing living can blossom into fruitage unless through nourishing stalks deep-planted in the common soil. The rose is merely the evidence of the vitality of the root; and the real source of its beauty, the very blush that it wears upon its tender cheek, comes from those silent sources of life that lie hidden in the chemistry of the soil. Up from that soil, up from the silent bosom of the earth, rise the currents of life and energy. Up from the common soil, up from the quiet heart of the people, rise joyously to-day streams of hope and determination bound to renew the face of the earth in glory.

I tell you, the so-called radicalism of our times is simply the effort of nature to release the generous energies of our people. This great American people is at bottom just, virtuous, and hopeful; the roots of its being are in the soil of what is lovely, pure, and of good report, and the need of the hour is just that radicalism that will clear a way for the realization of the aspirations of a sturdy race.

V

# THE PARLIAMENT OF THE PEOPLE

For a long time this country of ours has lacked one of the institutions which freemen have always and everywhere held fundamental. For a long time there has been no sufficient opportunity of counsel among the people; no place and method of talk, of exchange of opinion, of parley. Communities have outgrown the folk-moot and the town-meeting. Congress, in accordance with the genius of the land, which asks for action and is impatient of words,—Congress has become an institution which does its work in the privacy of committee rooms and not on the floor of the Chamber; a body that makes laws,—a legislature; not a body that debates, —not a parliament. Party conventions afford little or no opportunity for discussion; platforms are privately manufactured and adopted with a whoop. It is partly because citizens have foregone the taking of counsel together that the unholy alliances of bosses and Big Business have been able to assume to govern for us.

I conceive it to be one of the needs of the hour to restore the processes of common counsel, and to substitute them for the processes of private arrangement which now determine the policies of cities, states, and nation. We must learn, we freemen, to meet, as our fathers did, somehow, somewhere, for consultation. There must be discussion and debate, in which all freely participate.

It must be candid debate, and it must have for its honest purpose the clearing up of questions and the establishing of the truth. Too much political discussion is not to honest purpose, but only for the confounding of an opponent. I am often reminded, when political debate gets warm and we begin to hope that the truth is making inroads on the reason of those who have denied it, of the way a debate in Virginia once seemed likely to end:

When I was a young man studying at Charlottesville, there were two factions in the Democratic party in the State of Virginia which were having a pretty hot contest with each other. In one of the counties one of these factions had practically no following at all. A man named Massey, one of its redoubtable debaters, though a little, slim, insignificant-looking person, sent a messenger up into this county and challenged the opposition to debate with him. They didn't quite like the idea, but they were too proud to decline, so they put up their best debater, a big, good-natured man whom everybody was familiar with as "Tom," and it was arranged that Massey should have the first hour and that Tom Whatever-his-name-was should succeed him the next hour. When the occasion came, Massey, with his characteristic shrewdness, began to get underneath the skins of the audience, and he hadn't made more than half his speech before it was evident that he was getting that hostile crowd with him; whereupon one of Tom's partisans in the back of the room, seeing how things were going, cried out: "Tom, call him a liar and make it a fight!"

Now, that kind of debate, that spirit in discussion, gets us nowhere. Our national affairs are too serious, they lie too close to the well-being of each one of us, to excuse our talking about them except in earnestness and candor and a willingness to speak and listen with open minds. It is a misfortune that attends the party system that in the heat of a campaign partisan passions are so aroused that we cannot have frank discussion. Yet I am sure that I observe, and that all citizens must observe, an almost startling change in the temper of the people in this respect. The campaign just closed was markedly different from others that had preceded it in the degree to which party considerations were forgotten in the seriousness of the things we had to discuss as common citizens of an endangered country.

There is astir in the air of America something that I for one never saw before, never felt before. I have been going to political meetings all my life, though not all my life playing an immodestly conspicuous part in them; and there is a spirit in our political meetings now that I never saw before. It hasn't been very many years, let me say for example, that women attended political meetings. And women are attending political meetings now not simply because there is a woman question in politics; they are attending them because the modern political meeting is not like the political meeting of five or ten years ago. That was a mere ratification rally. That was a mere occasion for "whooping it up" for somebody. That was merely an occasion upon which one party was denounced unreasonably and the other was lauded unreasonably. No party has ever deserved quite the abuse that each party has got in turn, and nobody has ever deserved the praise that both parties have got in turn. The old political meeting was a wholly irrational performance; it was got together for the purpose of saying things that were chiefly not so and that were known by those who heard them not to be so, and were simply to be taken as a tonic in order to produce cheers.

But I am very much mistaken in the temper of my fellow-countrymen if the meetings I have seen in the last two years bear any resemblance to those older meetings. Men now get together in a political meeting in order to hear things of the deepest consequence discussed. And you will find almost as many Republicans in a Democratic meeting as you will find Democrats in a Republican meeting; the spirit of frank discussion, of common counsel, is abroad.

Good will it be for the country if the interest in public concerns manifested so widely and so sincerely be not suffered to expire with the election! Why should political debate go on only when somebody is to be elected? Why should it be confined to campaign time?

---

There is a movement on foot in which, in common with many men and women who love their country, I am greatly interested,—the movement to open the schoolhouse to the grown-up people in order that they may gather and talk over the affairs of the neighborhood and the state. There are schoolhouses all over the land which are not used by the teachers and children in the summer months, which are not used in the winter time in the evening for school purposes. These buildings belong to the public. Why not insist everywhere that they be used as places of discussion, such as of old took place in the town-meetings to which everybody went and where every public officer was freely called to account? The schoolhouse, which belongs to all of us, is a natural place in which to gather to consult over our common affairs.

I was very much interested in the remark of a fellow-citizen of ours who had been born on the other side of the water. He said that not long ago he wandered into one of those neighborhood schoolhouse meetings, and there found himself among people who were discussing matters in which they were all interested; and when he came out he said to me: "I have been living in America now ten years, and to-night for the first time I saw America as I had imagined it to be. This gathering together of men of all sorts upon a perfect footing of equality to discuss frankly with one another what concerned them all,—that is what I dreamed America was."

That set me to thinking. He hadn't seen the America he had come to find until that night. Had he not felt like a neighbor? Had men not consulted him? He had felt like an outsider. Had there been no little circles in which public affairs were discussed?

You know that the great melting-pot of America, the place where we are all made Americans of, is the public school, where men of every race and of every origin and of every station in life send their children, or ought to send their children, and where, being mixed together, the youngsters are all infused with the American spirit and developed into American men and American women. When, in addition to sending our children to school to paid teachers, we go to school to one another in those same schoolhouses, then we shall begin more fully to realize than we ever have realized before what American life is. And let me tell you this, confidentially, that wherever you find school boards that object to opening the schoolhouses in the evening for public meetings of every proper sort, you had better look around for some politician who is objecting to it; because the thing that cures bad politics is talk by the neighbors. The thing that brings to light the concealed circumstances of our political life is the talk of the neighborhood; and if you can get the neighbors together, get them frankly to tell everything they know, then your politics, your ward politics, and your city politics, and your state politics, too, will be turned inside out,—in the way they ought to be. Because the chief difficulty our politics has suffered is that the inside didn't look like the outside. Nothing clears the air like frank discussion.

One of the valuable lessons of my life was due to the fact that at a comparatively early age in my experience as a public speaker I had the privilege of speaking in Cooper Union in New York. The audience in Cooper Union is made up of every kind of man and woman, from the poor devil who simply comes in to keep warm up to the man who has come in to take a serious part in the discussion of the evening. I want to tell you this, that in the questions that are asked there after the speech is over, the most penetrating questions that I have ever had addressed to me came from some of the men who were the least well-dressed in the audience, came from the plain fellows, came from the fellows whose muscle was daily up against the whole struggle of life. They asked questions which went to the heart of the business and put me to my mettle to answer them. I felt as if those questions came as a voice out of life itself, not a voice out of any school less severe than the severe school of experience. And what I like about this social centre idea of the schoolhouse is that there is the place where the ordinary fellow is going to get his innings, going to ask his questions, going to express his opinions, going to convince those who do not realize the vigor of America that the vigor of America pulses in the blood of every true American, and that the only place he can find the true American is in this clearing-house of absolutely democratic opinion.

No one man understands the United States. I have met some gentlemen who professed they did. I have even met some business men who professed they held in their own single comprehension the business of the United States; but I am educated enough to know that they do not. Education has this useful effect, that it narrows of necessity the circles of one's egotism. No student knows his subject. The most he knows is where and how to find out the things he does not know with regard to it. That is also the position of a statesman. No statesman understands the whole country. He should make it his business to find out where he will get the information necessary to understand at least a part of it at a time when dealing with complex affairs. What we need is a universal revival of common counsel.

I have sometimes reflected on the lack of a body of public opinion in our cities, and once I contrasted the habits of the city man with those of the countryman in a way which got me into trouble. I described what a man in a city generally did when he got into a public vehicle or sat in a public place. He doesn't talk to anybody, but he plunges his head into a newspaper and presently experiences a reaction which he calls his opinion, but which is not an opinion at all, being merely the impression that a piece of news or an editorial has made upon him. He cannot be said to be participating in public opinion at all until he has laid his mind alongside the minds of his neighbors and discussed with them the incidents of the day and the tendencies of the time.

Where I got into trouble was, that I ventured on a comparison. I said that public opinion was not typified on the streets of a busy city, but was typified around the stove in a country store where men sat and probably chewed tobacco and spat into a sawdust box, and made up, before they got through, what was the neighborhood opinion both about persons and events; and then, inadvertently, I added this philosophical reflection, that, whatever might be said against the chewing of tobacco, this at least could be said for it: that it gave a man time to think between sentences. Ever since then I have been represented, particularly in the advertisements of tobacco firms, as in favor of the use of chewing tobacco!

The reason that some city men are not more catholic in their ideas is that they do not share the opinion of the country, and the reason that some countrymen are rustic is that they do not know the opinion of the city; they are both hampered by their limitations. I heard the other day of a woman who had lived all her life in a city and in an hotel. She made a first visit to the country last summer, and spent a week in a farmhouse. Asked afterward what had interested her most about her experience, she replied that it was hearing the farmer "page his cows!"

A very urban point of view with regard to a common rustic occurrence, and yet that language showed the sharp, the inelastic limits of her thought. She was provincial in the extreme; she thought even more narrowly than in the terms of a city; she thought in the terms of an hotel. In proportion as we are confined within the walls of one hostelry or one city or one state, we are provincial. We can do nothing more to advance our country's welfare than to bring the various communities within the counsels of the nation. The real difficulty of our nation has been that not enough of us realized that the matters we discussed were matters of common concern. We have talked as if we had to serve now this part of the country and again that part, now this interest and again that interest; as if all interests were not linked together, provided we understood them and knew how they were related to one another.

If you would know what makes the great river as it nears the sea, you must travel up the stream. You must go up into the hills and back into the forests and see the little rivulets, the little streams, all gathering in hidden places to swell the great body of water in the channel. And so with the making of public opinion: Back in the country, on the farms, in the shops, in the hamlets, in the homes of cities, in the schoolhouses, where men get together and are frank and true with one another, there come trickling down the streams which are to make the mighty force of the river, the river which is to drive all the enterprises of human life as it sweeps on into the great common sea of humanity.

I feel nothing so much as the intensity of the common man. I can pick out in any audience the men who are at ease in their fortunes: they are seeing a public man go through his stunts. But there are in every crowd other men who are not doing that,—men who are listening as if they were waiting to hear if there were somebody who could speak the thing that is stirring in their own hearts and minds. It makes a man's heart ache to think that he cannot be sure that he is doing it for them; to wonder whether they are longing for something that he does not understand. He prays God that something will bring into his consciousness what is in theirs, so that the whole nation may feel at last released from its dumbness, feel at last that there is no invisible force holding it back from its goal, feel at last that there is hope and confidence and that the road may be trodden as if we were brothers, shoulder to shoulder, not asking each other anything about differences of class, not contesting for any selfish advance, but united in the common enterprise.

The burden that is upon the heart of every conscientious public man is the burden of the thought that perhaps he does not sufficiently comprehend the national life. For, as a matter of fact, no single man does comprehend it. The whole purpose of democracy is that we may hold counsel with one another, so as not to depend upon the understanding of one man, but to depend upon the counsel of all. For only as men are brought into counsel, and state their own needs and interests, can the general interests of a great people be compounded into a policy that will be suitable to all.

I have realized all my life, as a man connected with the tasks of education, that the chief use of education is to open the understanding to comprehend as many things as possible. That it is not what a man knows,—for no man knows a great deal,—but what a man has upon his mind to find out; it is his ability to understand things, it is his connection with the great masses of men that makes him fit to speak for others,—and only that. I have associated with some of the gentlemen who are connected with the special interests of this country (and many of them are pretty fine men, I can tell you), but, fortunately for me, I have associated with a good many other persons besides; I have not confined my acquaintance to these interesting groups, and I can actually tell those gentlemen some things that they have not had time to find out. It has been my great good fortune not to have had my head buried in special undertakings, and, therefore, I have had an occasional look at the horizon. Moreover, I found out, a long time ago, fortunately for me, when I was a boy, that the United States did not consist of that part of it in which I lived. There was a time when I was a very narrow provincial, but happily the circumstances of my life made it necessary that I should go to a very distant part of the country, and I early found out what a very limited acquaintance I had with the United States, found out that the only thing that would give me any sense at all in discussing the affairs of the United States was to know as many parts of the United States as possible.

---

The men who have been ruling America must consent to let the majority into the game. We will no longer permit any system to go uncorrected which is based upon private understandings and expert testimony; we will not allow the few to continue to determine what the policy of the country is to be. It is a question of access to our own government. There are very few of us who have had any real access to the government. It ought to be a matter of common counsel; a matter of united counsel; a matter of mutual comprehension.

So, keep the air clear with constant discussion. Make every public servant feel that he is acting in the open and under scrutiny; and, above all things else, take these great fundamental questions of your lives with which political platforms concern themselves and search them through and through by every process of debate. Then we shall have a clear air in which we shall see our way to each kind of social betterment. When we have freed our government, when we have restored freedom of enterprise, when we have broken up the partnerships between money and power which now block us at every turn, then we shall see our way to accomplish all the handsome things which platforms promise in vain if they do not start at the point where stand the gates of liberty.

I am not afraid of the American people getting up and doing something. I am only afraid they will not; and when I hear a popular vote spoken of as mob government, I feel like telling the man who dares so to speak that he has no right to call himself an American. You cannot make a reckless, passionate force out of a body of sober people earning their living in a free country. Just picture to yourselves the voting population of this great land, from the sea to the far borders in the mountains, going calmly, man by man, to the polls, expressing its judgment about public affairs: is that your image of "a mob?"

What is a mob? A mob is a body of men in hot contact with one another, moved by ungovernable passion to do a hasty thing that they will regret the next day. Do you see anything resembling a mob in that voting population of the countryside, men tramping over the mountains, men going to the general store up in the village, men moving in little talking groups to the corner grocery to cast their ballots,—is that your notion of a mob? Or is that your picture of a free, self-governing people? I am not afraid of the judgments so expressed, if you give men time to think, if you give them a clear conception of the things they are to vote for; because the deepest conviction and passion of my heart is that the common people, by which I mean all of us, are to be absolutely trusted.

So, at this opening of a new age, in this its day of unrest and discontent, it is our part to clear the air, to bring about common counsel; to set up the parliament of the people; to demonstrate that we are fighting no man, that we are trying to bring all men to understand one another; that we are not the friends of any class against any other class, but that our duty is to make classes understand one another. Our part is to lift so high the incomparable standards of the common interest and the common justice that all men with vision, all men with hope, all men with the convictions of America in their hearts, will crowd to that standard and a new day of achievement may come for the liberty which we love.

# VI

# LET THERE BE LIGHT

The concern of patriotic men is to put our government again on its right basis, by substituting the popular will for the rule of guardians, the processes of common counsel for those of private arrangement. In order to do this, a first necessity is to open the doors and let in the light on all affairs which the people have a right to know about.

In the first place, it is necessary to open up all the processes of our politics. They have been too secret, too complicated, too roundabout; they have consisted too much of private conferences and secret understandings, of the control of legislation by men who were not legislators, but who stood outside and dictated, controlling oftentimes by very questionable means, which they would not have dreamed of allowing to become public. The whole process must be altered. We must take the selection of candidates for office, for example, out of the hands of small groups of men, of little coteries, out of the hands of machines working behind closed doors, and put it into the hands of the people themselves again by means of direct primaries and elections to which candidates of every sort and degree may have free access. We must substitute public for private machinery.

It is necessary, in the second place, to give society command of its own economic life again by denying to those who conduct the great modern operations of business the privacy that used to belong properly enough to men who used only their own capital and their individual energy in business. The processes of capital must be as open as the processes of politics. Those who make use of the great modern accumulations of wealth, gathered together by the dragnet process of the sale of stocks and bonds, and piling up of reserves, must be treated as under a public obligation; they must be made responsible for their business methods to the great communities which are in fact their working partners, so that the hand which makes correction shall easily reach them and a new principle of responsibility be felt throughout their structure and operation.

What are the right methods of politics? Why, the right methods are those of public discussion: the methods of leadership open and above board, not closeted with "boards of guardians" or anybody else, but brought out under the sky, where honest eyes can look upon them and honest eyes can judge of them.

If there is nothing to conceal, then why conceal it? If it is a public game, why play it in private? If it is a public game, then why not come out into the open and play it in public? You have got to cure diseased politics as we nowadays cure tuberculosis, by making all the people who suffer from it live out of doors; not only spend their days out of doors and walk around, but sleep out of doors; always remain in the open, where they will be accessible to fresh, nourishing, and revivifying influences.

I, for one, have the conviction that government ought to be all outside and no inside. I, for my part, believe that there ought to be no place where anything can be done that everybody does not know about. It would be very inconvenient for some gentlemen, probably, if government were all outside, but we have consulted their susceptibilities too long already. It is barely possible that some of these gentlemen are unjustly suspected; in that case they owe it to themselves to come out and operate in the light. The very fact that so much in politics is done in the dark, behind closed doors, promotes suspicion. Everybody knows that corruption thrives in secret places, and avoids public places, and we believe it a fair presumption that secrecy means impropriety. So, our honest politicians and our honorable corporation heads owe it to their reputations to bring their activities out into the open.

At any rate, whether they like it or not, these affairs are going to be dragged into the open. We are more anxious about their reputations than they are themselves. We are too solicitous for their morals,—if they are not,—to permit them longer to continue subject to the temptations of secrecy. You know there is temptation in loneliness and secrecy. Haven't you experienced it? I have. We are never so proper in our conduct as when everybody can look and see exactly what we are doing. If you are off in some distant part of the world and suppose that nobody who lives within a mile of your home is anywhere around, there are times when you adjourn your ordinary standards. You say to yourself: "Well, I'll have a fling this time; nobody will know anything about it." If you were on the desert of Sahara, you would feel that you might permit yourself,—well, say, some slight latitude in conduct; but if you saw one of your immediate neighbors coming the other way on a camel,—you would behave yourself until he got out of sight. The most dangerous thing in the world is to get off where nobody knows you. I advise you to stay around among the neighbors, and then you may keep out of jail. That is the only way some of us can keep out of jail.

Publicity is one of the purifying elements of politics. The best thing that you can do with anything that is crooked is to lift it up where people can see that it is crooked, and then it will either straighten itself out or disappear. Nothing checks all the bad practices of politics like public exposure. You can't be crooked in the light. I don't know whether it has ever been tried or not; but I venture to say, purely from observation, that it can't be done.

And so the people of the United States have made up their minds to do a healthy thing for both politics and big business. Permit me to mix a few metaphors: They are going to open doors; they are going to let up blinds; they are going to drag sick things into the open air and into the light of the sun. They are going to organize a great hunt, and smoke certain animals out of their burrows. They are going to unearth the beast in the jungle in which when they hunted they were caught by the beast instead of catching him. They have determined, therefore, to take an axe and raze the jungle, and then see where the beast will find cover. And I, for my part, bid them God-speed. The jungle breeds nothing but infection and shelters nothing but the enemies of mankind.

And nobody is going to get caught in our hunt except the beasts that prey. Nothing is going to be cut down or injured that anybody ought to wish preserved.

You know the story of the Irishman who, while digging a hole, was asked, "Pat, what are you doing,—digging a hole?" And he replied, "No, sir; I am digging the dirt, and laying the hole." It was probably the same Irishman who, seen digging around the wall of a house, was asked, "Pat, what are you doing?" And he answered, "Faith, I am letting the dark out of the cellar." Now, that's exactly what we want to do,—let the dark out of the cellar.

Take, first, the relations existing between politics and business.

It is perfectly legitimate, of course, that the business interests of the country should not only enjoy the protection of the law, but that they should be in every way furthered and strengthened and facilitated by legislation. The country has no jealousy of any connection between business and politics which is a legitimate connection. It is not in the least averse from open efforts to accommodate law to the material development which has so strengthened the country in all that it has undertaken by supplying its extraordinary life with its necessary physical foundations.

But the illegitimate connections between business and legislation are another matter. I would wish to speak on this subject with soberness and circumspection. I have no desire to excite anger against anybody. That would be easy, but it would do no particular good. I wish, rather, to consider an unhappy situation in a spirit that may enable us to account for it, to some extent, and so perhaps get at the causes and the remedy. Mere denunciation doesn't help much to clear up a matter so involved as is the complicity of business with evil politics in America.

Every community is vaguely aware that the political machine upon which it looks askance has certain very definite connections with men who are engaged in business on a large scale, and the suspicion which attaches to the machine itself has begun to attach also to business enterprises, just because these connections are known to exist. If these connections were open and avowed, if everybody knew just what they involved and just what use was being made of them, there would be no difficulty in keeping an eye upon affairs and in controlling them by public opinion. But, unfortunately, the whole process of law-making in America is a very obscure one. There is no highway of legislation, but there are many by-ways. Parties are not organized in such a way in our legislatures as to make any one group of men avowedly responsible for the course of legislation. The whole process of discussion, if any discussion at all takes place, is private and shut away from public scrutiny and knowledge. There are so many circles within circles, there are so many indirect and private ways of getting at legislative action, that our communities are constantly uneasy during legislative sessions. It is this confusion and obscurity and privacy of our legislative method that gives the political machine its opportunity. There is no publicly responsible man or group of men who are known to formulate legislation and to take charge of it from the time of its introduction until the time of its enactment. It has, therefore, been possible for an outside force,—the political machine, the body of men who nominated the legislators and who conducted the contest for their election,—to assume the rôle of control. Business men who desired something done in the way of changing the law under which they were acting, or who wished to prevent legislation which seemed to them to threaten their own interests, have known that there was this definite body of persons to resort to, and they have made terms with them. They have agreed to supply them with money for campaign expenses and to stand by them in all other cases where money was necessary if in return they might resort to them for protection or for assistance in matters of legislation. Legislators looked to a certain man who was not even a member of their body for instructions as to what they were to do with particular bills. The machine, which was the centre of party organization, was the natural instrument of control, and men who had business interests to promote naturally resorted to the body which exercised the control.

There need have been nothing sinister about this. If the whole matter had been open and candid and honest, public criticism would not have centred upon it. But the use of money always results in demoralization, and goes beyond demoralization to actual corruption. There are two kinds of corruption,—the crude and obvious sort, which consists in direct bribery, and the much subtler, more dangerous, sort, which consists in a corruption of the will. Business men who have tried to set up a control in politics through the machine have more and more deceived themselves, have allowed themselves to think that the whole matter was a necessary means of self-defence, have said that it was a necessary outcome of our political system. Having reassured themselves in this way, they have drifted from one thing to another until the questions of morals involved have become hopelessly obscured and submerged. How far away from the ideals of their youth have many of our men of business drifted, enmeshed in the vicious system,—how far away from the days when their fine young manhood was wrapped in "that chastity of honor which felt a stain like a wound!"

It is one of the happy circumstances of our time that the most intelligent of our business men have seen the mistake as well as the immorality of the whole bad business. The alliance between business and politics has been a burden to them,—an advantage, no doubt, upon occasion, but a very questionable and burdensome advantage. It has given them great power, but it has also subjected them to a sort of slavery and a bitter sort of subserviency to politicians. They are as anxious to be freed from bondage as the country is to be rid of the influences and methods which it represents. Leading business men are now becoming great factors in the emancipation of the country from a system which was leading from bad to worse. There are those, of course, who are wedded to the old ways and who will stand out for them to the last, but they will sink into a minority and be overcome. The rest have found that their old excuse (namely, that it was necessary to defend themselves against unfair legislation) is no longer a good excuse; that there is a better way of defending themselves than through the private use of money. That better way is to take the public into their confidence, to make absolutely open all their dealings with legislative bodies and legislative officers, and let the public judge as between them and those with whom they are dealing.

---

This discovery on their part of what ought to have been obvious all along points out the way of reform; for undoubtedly publicity comes very near being the cure-all for political and economic maladies of this sort. But publicity will continue to be very difficult so long as our methods of legislation are so obscure and devious and private. I think it will become more and more obvious that the way to purify our politics is to simplify them, and that the way to simplify them is to establish responsible leadership. We now have no leadership at all inside our legislative bodies, —at any rate, no leadership which is definite enough to attract the attention and watchfulness of the country. Our only leadership being that of irresponsible persons outside the legislatures who constitute the political machines, it is extremely difficult for even the most watchful public opinion to keep track of the circuitous methods pursued. This undoubtedly lies at the root of the growing demand on the part of American communities everywhere for responsible leadership, for putting in authority and keeping in authority those whom they know and whom they can watch and whom they can constantly hold to account. The business of the country ought to be served by thoughtful and progressive legislation, but it ought to be served openly, candidly, advantageously, with a careful regard to letting everybody be heard and every interest be considered, the interest which is not backed by money as well as the interest which is; and this can be accomplished only by some simplification of our methods which will centre the public trust in small groups of men who will lead, not by reason of legal authority, but by reason of their contact with and amenability to public opinion.

I am striving to indicate my belief that our legislative methods may well be reformed in the direction of giving more open publicity to every act, in the direction of setting up some form of responsible leadership on the floor of our legislative halls so that the people may know who is back of every bill and back of the opposition to it, and so that it may be dealt with in the open chamber rather than in the committee room. The light must be let in on all processes of law-making.

Legislation, as we nowadays conduct it, is not conducted in the open. It is not threshed out in open debate upon the floors of our assemblies. It is, on the contrary, framed, digested, and concluded in committee rooms. It is in committee rooms that legislation not desired by the interests dies. It is in committee rooms that legislation desired by the interests is framed and brought forth. There is not enough debate of it in open house, in most cases, to disclose the real meaning of the proposals made. Clauses lie quietly unexplained and unchallenged in our statutes which contain the whole gist and purpose of the act; qualifying phrases which escape the public attention, casual definitions which do not attract attention, classifications so technical as not to be generally understood, and which every one most intimately concerned is careful not to explain or expound, contain the whole purpose of the law. Only after it has been enacted and has come to adjudication in the courts is its scheme as a whole divulged. The beneficiaries are then safe behind their bulwarks.

Of course, the chief triumphs of committee work, of covert phrase and unexplained classification, are accomplished in the framing of tariffs. Ever since the passage of the outrageous Payne-Aldrich Tariff Act our people have been discovering the concealed meanings and purposes which lay hidden in it. They are discovering item by item how deeply and deliberately they were deceived and cheated. This did not happen by accident; it came about by design, by elaborated, secret design. Questions put upon the floor in the House and Senate were not frankly or truly answered, and an elaborate piece of legislation was foisted on the country which could not possibly have passed if it had been generally comprehended.

And we know, those of us who handle the machinery of politics, that the great difficulty in breaking up the control of the political boss is that he is backed by the money and the influence of these very people who are intrenched in these very schedules. The tariff could never have been built up item by item by public discussion, and it never could have passed, if item by item it had been explained to the people of this country. It was built up by arrangement and by the subtle management of a political organization represented in the Senate of the United States by the senior Senator from Rhode Island, and in the House of Representatives by one of the Representatives from Illinois. These gentlemen did not build that tariff upon the evidence that was given before the Committee on Ways and Means as to what the manufacturer and the workingmen, the consumers and the producers, of this country want. It was not built upon what the interests of the country called for. It was built upon understandings arrived at outside of the rooms where testimony was given and debate was held.

I am not even now suggesting corrupt influence. That is not my point. Corruption is a very difficult thing to manage in its literal sense. The payment of money is very easily detected, and men of this kind who control these interests by secret arrangement would not consent to receive a dollar in money. They are following their own principles,—that is to say, the principles which they think and act upon,—and they think that they are perfectly honorable and incorruptible men; but they believe one thing that I do not believe and that it is evident the people of the country do not believe: they believe that the prosperity of the country depends upon the arrangements which certain party leaders make with certain business leaders. They believe that, but the proposition has merely to be stated to the jury to be rejected. The prosperity of this country depends upon the interests of all of us and cannot be brought about by arrangement between any groups of persons. Take any question you like out to the country,—let it be threshed out in public debate,—and you will have made these methods impossible.

This is what sometimes happens: They promise you a particular piece of legislation. As soon as the legislature meets, a bill embodying that legislation is introduced. It is referred to a committee. You never hear of it again. What happened? Nobody knows what happened.

I am not intimating that corruption creeps in; I do not know what creeps in. The point is that we not only do not know, but it is intimated, if we get inquisitive, that it is none of our business. My reply is that it is our business, and it is the business of every man in the state; we have a right to know all the particulars of that bill's history. There is not any legitimate privacy about matters of government. Government must, if it is to be pure and correct in its processes, be absolutely public in everything that affects it. I cannot imagine a public man with a conscience having a secret that he would keep from the people about their own affairs.

I know how some of these gentlemen reason. They say that the influences to which they are yielding are perfectly legitimate influences, but that if they were disclosed they would not be understood. Well, I am very sorry, but nothing is legitimate that cannot be understood. If you cannot explain it properly, then there is something about it that cannot *be* explained at all. I know from the circumstances of the case, not what is happening, but that something private is happening, and that every time one of these bills gets into committee, something private stops it, and it never comes out again unless forced out by the agitation of the press or the courage and revolt of brave men in the legislature. I have known brave men of that sort. I could name some splendid examples of men who, as representatives of the people, demanded to be told by the chairman of the committee why the bill was not reported, and who, when they could not find out from him, investigated and found out for themselves and brought the bill out by threatening to tell the reason on the floor of the House.

Those are private processes. Those are processes which stand between the people and the things that are promised them, and I say that until you drive all of those things into the open, you are not connected with your government; you are not represented; you are not participants in your government. Such a scheme of government by private understanding deprives you of representation, deprives the people of representative institutions. It has got to be put into the heads of legislators that public business is public business. I hold the opinion that there can be no confidences as against the people with respect to their government, and that it is the duty of every public officer to explain to his fellow-citizens whenever he gets a chance,—explain exactly what is going on inside of his own office.

There is no air so wholesome as the air of utter publicity.

---

There are other tracts of modern life where jungles have grown up that must be cut down. Take, for example, the entirely illegitimate extensions made of the idea of private property for the benefit of modern corporations and trusts. A modern joint stock corporation cannot in any proper sense be said to base its rights and powers upon the principles of private property. Its powers are wholly derived from legislation. It possesses them for the convenience of business at the sufferance of the public. Its stock is widely owned, passes from hand to hand, brings multitudes of men into its shifting partnerships and connects it with the interests and the investments of whole communities. It is a segment of the public; bears no analogy to a partnership or to the processes by which private property is safeguarded and managed, and should not be suffered to afford any covert whatever to those who are managing it. Its management is of public and general concern, is in a very proper sense everybody's business. The business of many of those corporations which we call public-service corporations, and which are indispensable to our daily lives and serve us with transportation and light and water and power,—their business, for instance, is clearly public business; and, therefore, we can and must penetrate their affairs by the light of examination and discussion.

In New Jersey the people have realized this for a long time, and a year or two ago we got our ideas on the subject enacted into legislation. The corporations involved opposed the legislation with all their might. They talked about ruin,—and I really believe they did think they would be somewhat injured. But they have not been. And I hear I cannot tell you how many men in New Jersey say: "Governor, we were opposed to you; we did not believe in the things you wanted to do, but now that you have done them, we take off our hats. That was the thing to do, it did not hurt us a bit; it just put us on a normal footing; it took away suspicion from our business." New Jersey, having taken the cold plunge, cries out to the rest of the states, "Come on in! The water's fine!" I wonder whether these men who are controlling the government of the United States realize how they are creating every year a thickening atmosphere of suspicion, in which presently they will find that business cannot breathe?

So I take it to be a necessity of the hour to open up all the processes of politics and of public business,—open them wide to public view; to make them accessible to every force that moves, every opinion that prevails in the thought of the people; to give society command of its own economic life again, not by revolutionary measures, but by a steady application of the principle that the people have a right to look into such matters and to control them; to cut all privileges and patronage and private advantage and secret enjoyment out of legislation.

Wherever any public business is transacted, wherever plans affecting the public are laid, or enterprises touching the public welfare, comfort, or convenience go forward, wherever political programs are formulated, or candidates agreed on,—over that place a voice must speak, with the divine prerogative of a people's will, the words: "Let there be light!"

# VII

# THE TARIFF—"PROTECTION," OR SPECIAL PRIVILEGE?

Every business question, in this country, comes back, sooner or later, to the question of the tariff. You cannot escape from it, no matter in which direction you go. The tariff is situated in relation to other questions like Boston Common in the old arrangement of that interesting city. I remember seeing once, in *Life*, a picture of a man standing at the door of one of the railway stations in Boston and inquiring of a Bostonian the way to the Common. "Take any of these streets," was the reply, "in either direction." Now, as the Common was related to the winding streets of Boston, so the tariff question is related to the economic questions of our day. Take any direction and you will sooner or later get to the Common. And, in discussing the tariff you may start at the centre and go in any direction you please.

Let us illustrate by standing at the centre, the Common itself. As far back as 1828, when they knew nothing about "practical politics" as compared with what we know now, a tariff bill was passed which was called the "Tariff of Abominations," because it had no beginning nor end nor plan. It had no traceable pattern in it. It was as if the demands of everybody in the United States had all been thrown indiscriminately into one basket and that basket presented as a piece of legislation. It had been a general scramble and everybody who scrambled hard enough had been taken care of in the schedules resulting. It was an abominable thing to the thoughtful men of that day, because no man guided it, shaped it, or tried to make an equitable system out of it. That was bad enough, but at least everybody had an open door through which to scramble for his advantage. It was a go-as-you-please, free-for-all struggle, and anybody who could get to Washington and say he represented an important business interest could be heard by the Committee on Ways and Means.

We have a very different state of affairs now. The Committee on Ways and Means and the Finance Committee of the Senate in these sophisticated days have come to discriminate by long experience among the persons whose counsel they are to take in respect of tariff legislation. There has been substituted for the unschooled body of citizens that used to clamor at the doors of the Finance Committee and the Committee on Ways and Means, one of the most interesting and able bodies of expert lobbyists that has ever been developed in the experience of any country,—men who know so much about the matters they are talking of that you cannot put your knowledge into competition with theirs. They so overwhelm you with their familiarity with detail that you cannot discover wherein their scheme lies. They suggest the change of an innocent fraction in a particular schedule and explain it to you so plausibly that you cannot see that it means millions of dollars additional from the consumers of this country. They propose, for example, to put the carbon for electric lights in two-foot pieces instead of one-foot pieces,—and you do not see where you are getting sold, because you are not an expert. If you will get some expert to go through the schedules of the present Payne-Aldrich tariff, you will find a "nigger" concealed in almost every woodpile,—some little word, some little clause, some unsuspected item, that draws thousands of dollars out of the pockets of the consumer and yet does not seem to mean anything in particular. They have calculated the whole thing beforehand; they have analyzed the whole detail and consequence, each one in his specialty. With the tariff specialist the average business man has no possibility of competition. Instead of the old scramble, which was bad enough, we get the present expert control of the tariff schedules. Thus the relation between business and government becomes, not a matter of the exposure of all the sensitive parts of the government to all the active parts of the people, but the special impression upon them of a particular organized force in the business world.

Furthermore, every expedient and device of secrecy is brought into use to keep the public unaware of the arguments of the high protectionists, and ignorant of the facts which refute them; and uninformed of the intentions of the framers of the proposed legislation. It is notorious, even, that many members of the Finance Committee of the Senate did not know the significance of the tariff schedules which were reported in the present tariff bill to the Senate, and that members of the Senate who asked Mr. Aldrich direct questions were refused the information they sought; sometimes, I dare say, because he could not give it, and sometimes, I venture to say, because disclosure of the information would have embarrassed the passage of the measure. There were essential papers, moreover, which could not be got at.

---

Take that very interesting matter, that will-o'-the-wisp, known as "the cost of production." It is hard for any man who has ever studied economics at all to restrain a cynical smile when he is told that an intelligent group of his fellow-citizens are looking for "the cost of production" as a basis for tariff legislation. It is not the same in any one factory for two years together. It is not the same in one industry from one season to another. It is not the same in one country at two different epochs. It is constantly eluding your grasp. It nowhere exists, as a scientific, demonstrable fact. But, in order to carry out the pretences of the "protective" program, it was necessary to go through the motions of finding out what it was. I am credibly informed that the government of the United States requested several foreign governments, among others the government of Germany, to supply it with as reliable figures as possible concerning the cost of producing certain articles corresponding with those produced in the United States. The German government put the matter into the hands of certain of her manufacturers, who sent in just as complete answers as they could procure from their books. The information reached our government during the course of the debate on the Payne-Aldrich Bill and was transmitted,—for the bill by that time had reached the Senate,—to the Finance Committee of the Senate. But I am told,—and I have no reason to doubt it,—that it never came out of the pigeonholes of the committee. I don't know, and that committee doesn't know, what the information it contained was. When Mr. Aldrich was asked about it, he first said it was not an official report from the German government. Afterward he intimated that it was an impudent attempt on the part of the German government to interfere with tariff legislation in the United States. But he never said what the cost of production disclosed by it was. If he had, it is more than likely that some of the schedules would have been shown to be entirely unjustifiable.

Such instances show you just where the centre of gravity is,—and it is a matter of gravity indeed, for it is a very grave matter! It lay during the last Congress in the one person who was the accomplished intermediary between the expert lobbyists and the legislation of Congress. I am not saying this in derogation of the character of Mr. Aldrich. It is no concern of mine what kind of man Mr. Aldrich is; now, particularly, when he has retired from public life, is it a matter of indifference. The point is that he, because of his long experience, his long handling of these delicate and private matters, was the usual and natural instrument by which the Congress of the United States informed itself, not as to the wishes of the people of the United States or of the rank and file of business men of the country, but as to the needs and arguments of the experts who came to arrange matters with the committees.

The moral of the whole matter is this: The business of the United States is not as a whole in contact with the government of the United States. So soon as it is, the matters which now give you, and justly give you, cause for uneasiness will disappear. Just so soon as the business of this country has general, free, welcome access to the councils of Congress, all the friction between business and politics will disappear.

---

The tariff question is not the question that it was fifteen or twenty or thirty years ago. It used to be said by the advocates of the tariff that it made no difference even if there were a great wall separating us from the commerce of the world, because inside the United States there was so enormous an area of absolute free trade that competition within the country kept prices down to a normal level; that so long as one state could compete with all the others in the United States, and all the others compete with it, there would be only that kind of advantage gained which is gained by superior brain, superior economy, the better plant, the better administration; all of the things that have made America supreme, and kept prices in America down, because American genius was competing with American genius. I must add that so long as that was true, there was much to be said in defence of the protective tariff.

But the point now is that the protective tariff has been taken advantage of by some men to destroy domestic competition, to combine all existing rivals within our free-trade area, and to make it impossible for new men to come into the field. Under the high tariff there has been formed a network of factories which in their connection dominate the market of the United States and establish their own prices. Whereas, therefore, it was once arguable that the high tariff did not create the high cost of living, it is now no longer arguable that these combinations do not,—not by reason of the tariff, but by reason of their combination under the tariff,—settle what prices shall be paid; settle how much the product shall be; and settle, moreover, what shall be the market for labor.

The "protective" policy, as we hear it proclaimed to-day, bears no relation to the original doctrine enunciated by Webster and Clay. The "infant industries," which those statesmen desired to encourage, have grown up and grown gray, but they have always had new arguments for special favors. Their demands have gone far beyond what they dared ask for in the days of Mr. Blaine and Mr. McKinley, though both those apostles of "protection" were, before they died, ready to confess that the time had even then come to call a halt on the claims of the subsidized industries. William McKinley, before he died, showed symptoms of adjustment to the new age such as his successors have not exhibited. You remember what the utterances of Mr. McKinley's last month were with regard to the policy with which his name is particularly identified; I mean the policy of "protection." You remember how he joined in opinion with what Mr. Blaine before him had said—namely, that we had devoted the country to a policy which, too rigidly persisted in, was proving a policy of restriction; and that we must look forward to a time that ought to come very soon when we should enter into reciprocal relations of trade with all the countries of the world. This was another way of saying that we must substitute elasticity for rigidity; that we must substitute trade for closed ports. McKinley saw what his successors did not see. He saw that we had made for ourselves a strait-jacket.

When I reflect upon the "protective" policy of this country, and observe that it is the later aspects and the later uses of that policy which have built up trusts and monopoly in the United States, I make this contrast in my thought: Mr. McKinley had already uttered his protest against what he foresaw; his successor saw what McKinley had only foreseen, but he took no action. His successor saw those very special privileges, which Mr. McKinley himself began to suspect, used by the men who had obtained them to build up a monopoly for themselves, making freedom of enterprise in this country more and more difficult. I am one of those who have the utmost confidence that Mr. McKinley would not have sanctioned the later developments of the policy with which his name stands identified.

What is the present tariff policy of the protectionists? It is not the ancient protective policy to which I would give all due credit, but an entirely new doctrine. I ask anybody who is interested in the history of high "protective" tariffs to compare the latest platforms of the two "protective" tariff parties with the old doctrine. Men have been struck, students of this matter, by an entirely new departure. The new doctrine of the protectionist is that the tariff should represent the difference between the cost of production in America and the cost of production in other countries, *plus* a reasonable profit to those who are engaged in industry. This is the new part of the protective doctrine: "*plus* a reasonable profit." It openly guarantees profit to the men who come and ask favors of Congress. The old idea of a protective tariff was designed to keep American industries alive and, therefore, keep American labor employed. But the favors of protection have become so permanent that this is what has happened: Men, seeing that they need not fear foreign competition, have drawn together in great combinations. These combinations include factories (if it is a combination of factories) of all grades: old factories and new factories, factories with antiquated machinery and factories with brand-new machinery; factories that are economically and factories that are not economically administered; factories that have been long in the family, which have been allowed to run down, and factories with all the new modern inventions. As soon as the combination is effected the less efficient factories are generally put out of operation. But the stock issued in payment for them has to pay dividends. And the United States government guarantees profit on investment in factories that have gone out of business. As soon as these combinations see prices falling they reduce the hours of labor, they reduce production, they reduce wages, they throw men out of employment,—in order to do what? In order to keep the prices up in spite of their lack of efficiency.

There may have been a time when the tariff did not raise prices, but that time is past; the tariff is now taken advantage of by the great combinations in such a way as to give them control of prices. These things do not happen by chance. It does not happen by chance that prices are and have been rising faster here than in any other country. That river that divides us from Canada divides us from much cheaper living, notwithstanding that the Canadian Parliament levies duties on importations.

---

But "Ah!" exclaim those who do not understand what is going on; "you will ruin the country with your free trade!" Who said free trade? Who proposed free trade? You can't have free trade in the United States, because the government of the United States is of necessity, with our present division of the field of taxation between the federal and state governments, supported in large part by the duties collected at the ports. I should like to ask some gentlemen if very much is collected in the way of duties at the ports under the particular tariff schedules under which they operate. Some of the duties are practically prohibitive, and there is no tariff to be got from them.

When you buy an imported article, you pay a part of the price to the Federal government in the form of customs duty. But, as a rule, what you buy is, not the imported article, but a domestic article, the price of which the manufacturer has been able to raise to a point equal to, or higher than, the price of the foreign article *plus the duty*. But who gets the tariff tax in this case? The government? Oh, no; not at all. The manufacturer. The American manufacturer, who says that while he can't sell goods as low as the foreign manufacturer, all good Americans ought to buy of him and pay him a tax on every article for the privilege. Perhaps we ought. The original idea was that, when he was just starting and needed support, we ought to buy of him, even if we had to pay a higher price, till he could get on his feet. Now it is said that we ought to buy of him and pay him a price 15 to 120 per cent. higher than we need pay the foreign manufacturer, even if he is a six-foot, bearded "infant," because the cost of production is necessarily higher here than anywhere else. I don't know why it should be. The American workingman used to be able to do so much more and better work than the foreigner that that more than compensated for his higher wages and made him a good bargain at any wage.

Of course, if we are going to agree to give any fellow-citizen who takes a notion to go into some business or other for which the country is not especially adapted,—if we are going to give him a bonus on every article he produces big enough to make up for the handicap he labors under because of some natural reason or other,—why, we may indeed gloriously diversify our industries, but we shall beggar ourselves. On this principle, we shall have in Connecticut, or Michigan, or somewhere else, miles of hothouses in which thousands of happy American workingmen, with full dinner-pails, will be raising bananas,—to be sold at a quarter apiece. Some foolish person, a benighted Democrat like as not, might timidly suggest that bananas were a greater public blessing when they came from Jamaica and were three for a nickel, but what patriotic citizen would listen for a moment to the criticisms of a person without any conception of the beauty and glory of the great American banana industry, without realization of the proud significance of the fact that Old Glory floats over the biggest banana hothouses in the world!

But that is a matter on one side. What I am trying to point out to you now is that this "protective" tariff, so-called, has become a means of fostering the growth of particular groups of industry at the expense of the economic vitality of the rest of the country. What the people now propose is a very practical thing indeed: They propose to unearth these special privileges and to cut them out of the tariff. They propose not to leave a single concealed private advantage in the statutes concerning the duties that can possibly be eradicated without affecting the part of the business that is sound and legitimate and which we all wish to see promoted.

Some men talk as if the tariff-reformers, as if the Democrats, weren't part of the United States. I met a lady the other day, not an elderly lady, who said to me with pride: "Why, I have been a Democrat ever since they hunted them with dogs." And you would really suppose, to hear some men talk, that Democrats were outlaws and did not share the life of the United States. Why, Democrats constitute nearly one half the voters of this country. They are engaged in all sorts of enterprises, big and little. There isn't a walk of life or a kind of occupation in which you won't find them; and, as a Philadelphia paper very wittily said the other day, they can't commit economic murder without committing economic suicide. Do you suppose, therefore, that half of the population of the United States is going about to destroy the very foundations of our economic life by simply running amuck amidst the schedules of the tariff? Some of the schedules are so tough that they wouldn't be hurt, if it did. But that isn't the program, and anybody who says that it is simply doesn't understand the situation at all. All that the tariff-reformers claim is this: that the partnership ought to be bigger than it is. Just because there are so many of them, they know how many are outside. And let me tell you, just as many Republicans are outside. The only thing I have against my protectionist fellow-citizens is that they have allowed themselves to be imposed upon so many years. Think of saying that the "protective" tariff is for the benefit of the workingman, in the presence of all those facts that have just been disclosed in Lawrence, Mass., where the worst schedule of all—"Schedule K"—operates to keep men on wages on which they cannot live. Why, the audacity, the impudence, of the claim is what strikes one; and in face of the fact that the workingmen of this country who are in unprotected industries are better paid than those who are in "protected" industries; at any rate, in the conspicuous industries! The Steel schedule, I dare say, is rather satisfactory to those who manufacture steel, but is it satisfactory to those who make the steel with their own tired hands? Don't you know that there are mills in which men are made to work seven days in the week for twelve hours a day, and in the three hundred and sixty-five weary days of the year can't make enough to pay their bills? And this in one of the giants among our industries, one of the undertakings which have thriven to gigantic size upon this very system.

Ah, the whole mass of the fraud is falling away, and men are beginning to see disclosed little groups of persons maintaining a control over the dominant party and through the dominant party over the government, in their own interest, and not in the interest of the people of the United States!

---

Let me repeat: There cannot be free trade in the United States so long as the established fiscal policy of the federal government is maintained. The federal government has chosen throughout all the generations that have preceded us to maintain itself chiefly on indirect instead of direct taxation. I dare say we shall never see a time when it can alter that policy in any substantial degree; and there is no Democrat of thoughtfulness that I have met who contemplates a program of free trade.

But what we intend to do, what the House of Representatives has been attempting to do and will attempt to do again, and succeed in doing, is to weed this garden that we have been cultivating. Because, if we have been laying at the roots of our industrial enterprises this fertilization of protection, if we have been stimulating it by this policy, we have found that the stimulation was not equal in respect of all the growths in the garden, and that there are some growths, which every man can distinguish with the naked eye, which have so overtopped the rest, which have so thrown the rest into destroying shadow, that it is impossible for the industries of the United States as a whole to prosper under their blighting shade. In other words, we have found out that this that professes to be a process of protection has become a process of favoritism, and that the favorites of this policy have flourished at the expense of all the rest. And now we are going into this garden and weed it. We are going into this garden and give the little plants air and light in which to grow. We are going to pull up every root that has so spread itself as to draw the nutriment of the soil from the other roots. We are going in there to see to it that the fertilization of intelligence, of invention, of origination, is once more applied to a set of industries now threatening to be stagnant, because threatening to be too much concentrated. The policy of freeing the country from the restrictive tariff will so variegate and multiply the undertakings in the country that there will be a wider market and a greater competition for labor; it will let the sun shine through the clouds again as once it shone on the free, independent, unpatronized intelligence and energy of a great people.

One of the counts of the indictment against the so-called "protective" tariff is that it has robbed Americans of their independence, resourcefulness, and self-reliance. Our industry has grown invertebrate, cowardly, dependent on government aid. When I hear the argument of some of the biggest business men in this country, that if you took the "protection" of the tariff off they would be overcome by the competition of the world, I ask where and when it happened that the boasted genius of America became afraid to go out into the open and compete with the world? Are we children, are we wards, are we still such puerile infants that we have to be fed out of a bottle? Isn't it true that we know how to make steel in America better than anybody else in the world? Yet they say, "For Heaven's sake don't expose us to the chill of prices coming from any other quarter of the globe." Mind you, we can compete with those prices. Steel is sold abroad, steel made in America is sold abroad in many of its forms, much cheaper than it is sold in America. It is so hard for people to get that into their heads!

We set up a kindergarten in New York. We called it the Chamber of Horrors. We exhibited there a great many things manufactured in the United States, with the prices at which they were sold in the United States, and the prices at which they were sold outside of the United States, marked on them. If you tell a woman that she can buy a sewing machine for eighteen dollars in Mexico that she has to pay thirty dollars for in the United States, she will not heed it or she will forget it unless you take her and show her the machine with the price marked on it. My very distinguished friend, Senator Gore, of Oklahoma, made this interesting proposal: that we should pass a law that every piece of goods sold in the United States should have on it a label bearing the price at which it sells under the tariff and the price at which it would sell if there were no tariff, and then the Senator suggests that we have a very easy solution for the tariff question. He does not want to oblige that great body of our fellow-citizens who have a conscientious belief in "protection" to turn away from it. He proposes that everybody who believes in the "protective" tariff should pay it and the rest of us should not; if they want to subscribe, it is open to them to subscribe.

As for the rest of us, the time is coming when we shall not have to subscribe. The people of this land have made up their minds to cut all privilege and patronage out of our fiscal legislation, particularly out of that part of it which affects the tariff. We have come to recognize in the tariff as it is now constructed, not a system of protection, but a system of favoritism, of privilege, too often granted secretly and by subterfuge, instead of openly and frankly and legitimately, and we have determined to put an end to the whole bad business, not by hasty and drastic changes, but by the adoption of an entirely new principle,—by the reformation of the whole purpose of legislation of that kind. We mean that our tariff legislation henceforth shall have as its object, not private profit, but the general public development and benefit. We shall make our fiscal laws, not like those who dole out favors, but like those who serve a nation. We are going to begin with those particular items where we find special privilege intrenched. We know what those items are; these gentlemen have been kind enough to point them out themselves. What we are interested in first of all with regard to the tariff is getting the grip of special interests off the throat of Congress. We do not propose that special interests shall any longer camp in the rooms of the Committee on Ways and Means of the House and the Finance Committee of the Senate. We mean that those shall be places where the people of the United States shall come and be represented, in order that everything may be done in the general interest, and not in the interest of particular groups of persons who already dominate the industries and the industrial development of this country. Because no matter how wise these gentlemen may be, no matter how patriotic, no matter how singularly they may be gifted with the power to divine the right courses of business, there isn't any group of men in the United States or in any other country who are wise enough to have the destinies of a great people put into their hands as trustees. We mean that business in this land shall be released, emancipated.

# VIII

# MONOPOLY, OR OPPORTUNITY?

Gentlemen say, they have been saying for a long time, and, therefore, I assume that they believe, that trusts are inevitable. They don't say that big business is inevitable. They don't say merely that the elaboration of business upon a great co-operative scale is characteristic of our time and has come about by the natural operation of modern civilization. We would admit that. But they say that the particular kind of combinations that are now controlling our economic development came into existence naturally and were inevitable; and that, therefore, we have to accept them as unavoidable and administer our development through them. They take the analogy of the railways. The railways were clearly inevitable if we were to have transportation, but railways after they are once built stay put. You can't transfer a railroad at convenience; and you can't shut up one part of it and work another part. It is in the nature of what economists, those tedious persons, call natural monopolies; simply because the whole circumstances of their use are so stiff that you can't alter them. Such are the analogies which these gentlemen choose when they discuss the modern trust.

I admit the popularity of the theory that the trusts have come about through the natural development of business conditions in the United States, and that it is a mistake to try to oppose the processes by which they have been built up, because those processes belong to the very nature of business in our time, and that therefore the only thing we can do, and the only thing we ought to attempt to do, is to accept them as inevitable arrangements and make the best out of it that we can by regulation.

I answer, nevertheless, that this attitude rests upon a confusion of thought. Big business is no doubt to a large extent necessary and natural. The development of business upon a great scale, upon a great scale of co-operation, is inevitable, and, let me add, is probably desirable. But that is a very different matter from the development of trusts, because the trusts have not grown. They have been artificially created; they have been put together, not by natural processes, but by the will, the deliberate planning will, of men who were more powerful than their neighbors in the business world, and who wished to make their power secure against competition.

The trusts do not belong to the period of infant industries. They are not the products of the time, that old laborious time, when the great continent we live on was undeveloped, the young nation struggling to find itself and get upon its feet amidst older and more experienced competitors. They belong to a very recent and very sophisticated age, when men knew what they wanted and knew how to get it by the favor of the government.

Did you ever look into the way a trust was made? It is very natural, in one sense, in the same sense in which human greed is natural. If I haven't efficiency enough to beat my rivals, then the thing I am inclined to do is to get together with my rivals and say: "Don't let's cut each other's throats; let's combine and determine prices for ourselves; determine the output, and thereby determine the prices: and dominate and control the market." That is very natural. That has been done ever since freebooting was established. That has been done ever since power was used to establish control. The reason that the masters of combination have sought to shut out competition is that the basis of control under competition is brains and efficiency. I admit that any large corporation built up by the legitimate processes of business, by economy, by efficiency, is natural; and I am not afraid of it, no matter how big it grows. It can stay big only by doing its work more thoroughly than anybody else. And there is a point of bigness,—as every business man in this country knows, though some of them will not admit it, —where you pass the limit of efficiency and get into the region of clumsiness and unwieldiness. You can make your combine so extensive that you can't digest it into a single system; you can get so many parts that you can't assemble them as you would an effective piece of machinery. The point of efficiency is overstepped in the natural process of development oftentimes, and it has been overstepped many times in the artificial and deliberate formation of trusts.

A trust is formed in this way: a few gentlemen "promote" it—that is to say, they get it up, being given enormous fees for their kindness, which fees are loaded on to the undertaking in the form of securities of one kind or another. The argument of the promoters is, not that every one who comes into the combination can carry on his business more efficiently than he did before; the argument is: we will assign to you as your share in the pool twice, three times, four times, or five times what you could have sold your business for to an individual competitor who would have to run it on an economic and competitive basis. We can afford to buy it at such a figure because we are shutting out competition. We can afford to make the stock of the combination half a dozen times what it naturally would be and pay dividends on it, because there will be nobody to dispute the prices we shall fix.

Talk of that as sound business? Talk of that as inevitable? It is based upon nothing except power. It is not based upon efficiency. It is no wonder that the big trusts are not prospering in proportion to such competitors as they still have in such parts of their business as competitors have access to; they are prospering freely only in those fields to which competition has no access. Read the statistics of the Steel Trust, if you don't believe it. Read the statistics of any trust. They are constantly nervous about competition, and they are constantly buying up new competitors in order to narrow the field. The United States Steel Corporation is gaining in its supremacy in the American market only with regard to the cruder manufactures of iron and steel, but wherever, as in the field of more advanced manufactures of iron and steel, it has important competitors, its portion of the product is not increasing, but is decreasing, and its competitors, where they have a foothold, are often more efficient than it is.

Why? Why, with unlimited capital and innumerable mines and plants everywhere in the United States, can't they beat the other fellows in the market? Partly because they are carrying too much. Partly because they are unwieldy. Their organization is imperfect. They bought up inefficient plants along with efficient, and they have got to carry what they have paid for, even if they have to shut some of the plants up in order to make any interest on their investments; or, rather, not interest on their investments, because that is an incorrect word,—on their alleged capitalization. Here we have a lot of giants staggering along under an almost intolerable weight of artificial burdens, which they have put on their own backs, and constantly looking about lest some little pigmy with a round stone in a sling may come out and slay them.

For my part, I want the pigmy to have a chance to come out. And I foresee a time when the pigmies will be so much more athletic, so much more astute, so much more active, than the giants, that it will be a case of Jack the giant-killer. Just let some of the youngsters I know have a chance and they'll give these gentlemen points. Lend them a little money. They can't get any now. See to it that when they have got a local market they can't be squeezed out of it. Give them a chance to capture that market and then see them capture another one and another one, until these men who are carrying an intolerable load of artificial securities find that they have got to get down to hard pan to keep their foothold at all. I am willing to let Jack come into the field with the giant, and if Jack has the brains that some Jacks that I know in America have, then I should like to see the giant get the better of him, with the load that he, the giant, has to carry,—the load of water. For I'll undertake to put a water-logged giant out of business any time, if you will give me a fair field and as much credit as I am entitled to, and let the law do what from time immemorial law has been expected to do,—see fair play.

As for watered stock, I know all the sophistical arguments, and they are many, for capitalizing earning capacity. It is a very attractive and interesting argument, and in some instances it is legitimately used. But there is a line you cross, above which you are not capitalizing your earning capacity, but capitalizing your control of the market, capitalizing the profits which you got by your control of the market, and didn't get by efficiency and economy. These things are not hidden even from the layman. These are not half-hidden from college men. The college men's days of innocence have passed, and their days of sophistication have come. They know what is going on, because we live in a talkative world, full of statistics, full of congressional inquiries, full of trials of persons who have attempted to live independently of the statutes of the United States; and so a great many things have come to light under oath, which we must believe upon the credibility of the witnesses who are, indeed, in many instances very eminent and respectable witnesses.

I take my stand absolutely, where every progressive ought to take his stand, on the proposition that private monopoly is indefensible and intolerable. And there I will fight my battle. And I know how to fight it. Everybody who has even read the newspapers knows the means by which these men built up their power and created these monopolies. Any decently equipped lawyer can suggest to you statutes by which the whole business can be stopped. What these gentlemen do not want is this: they do not want to be compelled to meet all comers on equal terms. I am perfectly willing that they should beat any competitor by fair means; but I know the foul means they have adopted, and I know that they can be stopped by law. If they think that coming into the market upon the basis of mere efficiency, upon the mere basis of knowing how to manufacture goods better than anybody else and to sell them cheaper than anybody else, they can carry the immense amount of water that they have put into their enterprises in order to buy up rivals, then they are perfectly welcome to try it. But there must be no squeezing out of the beginner, no crippling his credit; no discrimination against retailers who buy from a rival; no threats against concerns who sell supplies to a rival; no holding back of raw material from him; no secret arrangements against him. All the fair competition you choose, but no unfair competition of any kind. And then when unfair competition is eliminated, let us see these gentlemen carry their tanks of water on their backs. All that I ask and all I shall fight for is that they shall come into the field against merit and brains everywhere. If they can beat other American brains, then they have got the best brains.

But if you want to know how far brains go, as things now are, suppose you try to match your better wares against these gentlemen, and see them undersell you before your market is any bigger than the locality and make it absolutely impossible for you to get a fast foothold. If you want to know how brains count, originate some invention which will improve the kind of machinery they are using, and then see if you can borrow enough money to manufacture it. You may be offered something for your patent by the corporation,—which will perhaps lock it up in a safe and go on using the old machinery; but you will not be allowed to manufacture. I know men who have tried it, and they could not get the money, because the great money lenders of this country are in the arrangement with the great manufacturers of this country, and they do not propose to see their control of the market interfered with by outsiders. And who are outsiders? Why, all the rest of the people of the United States are outsiders.

They are rapidly making us outsiders with respect even of the things that come from the bosom of the earth, and which belong to us in a peculiar sense. Certain monopolies in this country have gained almost complete control of the raw material, chiefly in the mines, out of which the great body of manufactures are carried on, and they now discriminate, when they will, in the sale of that raw material between those who are rivals of the monopoly and those who submit to the monopoly. We must soon come to the point where we shall say to the men who own these essentials of industry that they have got to part with these essentials by sale to all citizens of the United States with the same readiness and upon the same terms. Or else we shall tie up the resources of this country under private control in such fashion as will make our independent development absolutely impossible.

There is another injustice that monopoly engages in. The trust that deals in the cruder products which are to be transformed into the more elaborate manufactures often will not sell these crude products except upon the terms of monopoly,—that is to say, the people that deal with them must buy exclusively from them. And so again you have the lines of development tied up and the connections of development knotted and fastened so that you cannot wrench them apart.

Again, the manufacturing monopolies are so interlaced in their personal relationships with the great shipping interests of this country, and with the great railroads, that they can often largely determine the rates of shipment.

The people of this country are being very subtly dealt with. You know, of course, that, unless our Commerce Commissions are absolutely sleepless, you can get rebates without calling them such at all. The most complicated study I know of is the classification of freight by the railway company. If I wanted to make a special rate on a special thing, all I should have to do is to put it in a special class in the freight classification, and the trick is done. And when you reflect that the twenty-four men who control the United States Steel Corporation, for example, are either presidents or vice-presidents or directors in 55 per cent. of the railways of the United States, reckoning by the valuation of those railroads and the amount of their stock and bonds, you know just how close the whole thing is knitted together in our industrial system, and how great the temptation is. These twenty-four gentlemen administer that corporation as if it belonged to them. The amazing thing to me is that the people of the United States have not seen that the administration of a great business like that is not a private affair; it is a public affair.

I have been told by a great many men that the idea I have, that by restoring competition you can restore industrial freedom, is based upon a failure to observe the actual happenings of the last decades in this country; because, they say, it is just free competition that has made it possible for the big to crush the little.

I reply, it is not free competition that has done that; it is illicit competition. It is competition of the kind that the law ought to stop, and can stop,—this crushing of the little man.

You know, of course, how the little man is crushed by the trusts. He gets a local market. The big concerns come in and undersell him in his local market, and that is the only market he has; if he cannot make a profit there, he is killed. They can make a profit all through the rest of the Union, while they are underselling him in his locality, and recouping themselves by what they can earn elsewhere. Thus their competitors can be put out of business, one by one, wherever they dare to show a head. Inasmuch as they rise up only one by one, these big concerns can see to it that new competitors never come into the larger field. You have to begin somewhere. You can't begin in space. You can't begin in an airship. You have got to begin in some community. Your market has got to be your neighbors first and those who know you there. But unless you have unlimited capital (which of course you wouldn't have when you were beginning) or unlimited credit (which these gentlemen can see to it that you shan't get), they can kill you out in your local market any time they try, on the same basis exactly as that on which they beat organized labor; for they can sell at a loss in your market because they are selling at a profit everywhere else, and they can recoup the losses by which they beat you by the profits which they make in fields where they have beaten other fellows and put them out. If ever a competitor who by good luck has plenty of money does break into the wider market, then the trust has to buy him out, paying three or four times what the business is worth. Following such a purchase it has got to pay the interest on the price it has paid for the business, and it has got to tax the whole people of the United States, in order to pay the interest on what it borrowed to do that, or on the stocks and bonds it issued to do it with. Therefore the big trusts, the big combinations, are the most wasteful, the most uneconomical, and, after they pass a certain size, the most inefficient, way of conducting the industries of this country.

A notable example is the way in which Mr. Carnegie was bought out of the steel business. Mr. Carnegie could build better mills and make better steel rails and make them cheaper than anybody else connected with what afterward became the United States Steel Corporation. They didn't dare leave him outside. He had so much more brains in finding out the best processes; he had so much more shrewdness in surrounding himself with the most successful assistants; he knew so well when a young man who came into his employ was fit for promotion and was ripe to put at the head of some branch of his business and was sure to make good, that he could undersell every mother's son of them in the market for steel rails. And they bought him out at a price that amounted to three or four times,—I believe actually five times,—the estimated value of his properties and of his business, because they couldn't beat him in competition. And then in what they charged afterward for their product,—the product of his mills included, —they made us pay the interest on the four or five times the difference.

That is the difference between a big business and a trust. A trust is an arrangement to get rid of competition, and a big business is a business that has survived competition by conquering in the field of intelligence and economy. A trust does not bring efficiency to the aid of business; it *buys efficiency out of business*. I am for big business, and I am against the trusts. Any man who can survive by his brains, any man who can put the others out of the business by making the thing cheaper to the consumer at the same time that he is increasing its intrinsic value and quality, I take off my hat to, and I say: "You are the man who can build up the United States, and I wish there were more of you."

There will not be more, unless we find a way to prevent monopoly. You know perfectly well that a trust business staggering under a capitalization many times too big is not a business that can afford to admit competitors into the field; because the minute an economical business, a business with its capital down to hard pan, with every ounce of its capital working, comes into the field against such an overloaded corporation, it will inevitably beat it and undersell it; therefore it is to the interest of these gentlemen that monopoly be maintained. They cannot rule the markets of the world in any way but by monopoly. It is not surprising to find them helping to found a new party with a fine program of benevolence, but also with a tolerant acceptance of monopoly.

---

There is another matter to which we must direct our attention, whether we like or not. I do not take these things into my mouth because they please my palate; I do not talk about them because I want to attack anybody or upset anything; I talk about them because only by open speech about them among ourselves shall we learn what the facts are.

You will notice from a recent investigation that things like this take place: A certain bank invests in certain securities. It appears from evidence that the handling of these securities was very intimately connected with the maintenance of the price of a particular commodity. Nobody ought, and in normal circumstances nobody would, for a moment think of suspecting the managers of a great bank of making such an investment in order to help those who were conducting a particular business in the United States maintain the price of their commodity; but the circumstances are not normal. It is beginning to be believed that in the big business of this country nothing is disconnected from anything else. I do not mean in this particular instance to which I have referred, and I do not have in mind to draw any inference at all, for that would be unjust; but take any investment of an industrial character by a great bank. It is known that the directorate of that bank interlaces in personnel with ten, twenty, thirty, forty, fifty, sixty boards of directors of all sorts, of railroads which handle commodities, of great groups of manufacturers which manufacture commodities, and of great merchants who distribute commodities; and the result is that every great bank is under suspicion with regard to the motive of its investments. It is at least considered possible that it is playing the game of somebody who has nothing to do with banking, but with whom some of its directors are connected and joined in interest. The ground of unrest and uneasiness, in short, on the part of the public at large, is the growing knowledge that many large undertakings are interlaced with one another, are indistinguishable from one another in personnel.

Therefore, when a small group of men approach Congress in order to induce the committee concerned to concur in certain legislation, nobody knows the ramifications of the interests which those men represent; there seems no frank and open action of public opinion in public counsel, but every man is suspected of representing some other man and it is not known where his connections begin or end.

I am one of those who have been so fortunately circumstanced that I have had the opportunity to study the way in which these things come about in complete disconnection from them, and I do not suspect that any man has deliberately planned the system. I am not so uninstructed and misinformed as to suppose that there is a deliberate and malevolent combination somewhere to dominate the government of the United States. I merely say that, by certain processes, now well known, and perhaps natural in themselves, there has come about an extraordinary and very sinister concentration in the control of business in the country.

However it has come about, it is more important still that the control of credit also has become dangerously centralized. It is the mere truth to say that the financial resources of the country are not at the command of those who do not submit to the direction and domination of small groups of capitalists who wish to keep the economic development of the country under their own eye and guidance. The great monopoly in this country is the monopoly of big credits. So long as that exists, our old variety and freedom and individual energy of development are out of the question. A great industrial nation is controlled by its system of credit. Our system of credit is privately concentrated. The growth of the nation, therefore, and all our activities are in the hands of a few men who, even if their action be honest and intended for the public interest, are necessarily concentrated upon the great undertakings in which their own money is involved and who necessarily, by very reason of their own limitations, chill and check and destroy genuine economic freedom. This is the greatest question of all, and to this statesmen must address themselves with an earnest determination to serve the long future and the true liberties of men.

This money trust, or, as it should be more properly called, this credit trust, of which Congress has begun an investigation, is no myth; it is no imaginary thing. It is not an ordinary trust like another. It doesn't do business every day. It does business only when there is occasion to do business. You can sometimes do something large when it isn't watching, but when it is watching, you can't do much. And I have seen men squeezed by it; I have seen men who, as they themselves expressed it, were put "out of business by Wall Street," because Wall Street found them inconvenient and didn't want their competition.

Let me say again that I am not impugning the motives of the men in Wall Street. They may think that that is the best way to create prosperity for the country. When you have got the market in your hand, does honesty oblige you to turn the palm upside down and empty it? If you have got the market in your hand and believe that you understand the interest of the country better than anybody else, is it patriotic to let it go? I can imagine them using this argument to themselves.

The dominating danger in this land is not the existence of great individual combinations,—that is dangerous enough in all conscience,—but the combination of the combinations,—of the railways, the manufacturing enterprises, the great mining projects, the great enterprises for the development of the natural water-powers of the country, threaded together in the personnel of a series of boards of directors into a "community of interest" more formidable than any conceivable single combination that dare appear in the open.

The organization of business has become more centralized, vastly more centralized, than the political organization of the country itself. Corporations have come to cover greater areas than states; have come to live under a greater variety of laws than the citizen himself, have excelled states in their budgets and loomed bigger than whole commonwealths in their influence over the lives and fortunes of entire communities of men. Centralized business has built up vast structures of organization and equipment which overtop all states and seem to have no match or competitor except the federal government itself.

What we have got to do,—and it is a colossal task not to be undertaken with a light head or without judgment,—what we have got to do is to disentangle this colossal "community of interest." No matter how we may purpose dealing with a single combination in restraint of trade, you will agree with me in this, that no single, avowed, combination is big enough for the United States to be afraid of; but when all the combinations are combined and this final combination is not disclosed by any process of incorporation or law, but is merely an identity of personnel, or of interest, then there is something that even the government of the nation itself might come to fear,—something for the law to pull apart, and gently, but firmly and persistently, dissect.

You know that the chemist distinguishes between a chemical combination and an amalgam. A chemical combination has done something which I cannot scientifically describe, but its molecules have become intimate with one another and have practically united, whereas an amalgam has a mere physical union created by pressure from without. Now, you can destroy that mere physical contact without hurting the individual elements, and this community of interest is an amalgam; you can break it up without hurting any one of the single interests combined. Not that I am particularly delicate of some of the interests combined,—I am not under bonds to be unduly polite to them,—but I am interested in the business of the country, and believe its integrity depends upon this dissection. I do not believe any one group of men has vision enough or genius enough to determine what the development of opportunity and the accomplishment by achievement shall be in this country.

The facts of the situation amount to this: that a comparatively small number of men control the raw material of this country; that a comparatively small number of men control the water-powers that can be made useful for the economical production of the energy to drive our machinery; that that same number of men largely control the railroads; that by agreements handed around among themselves they control prices, and that that same group of men control the larger credits of the country.

---

When we undertake the strategy which is going to be necessary to overcome and destroy this far-reaching system of monopoly, we are rescuing the business of this country, we are not injuring it; and when we separate the interests from each other and dismember these communities of connection, we have in mind a greater community of interest, a vaster community of interest, the community of interest that binds the virtues of all men together, that community of mankind which is broad and catholic enough to take under the sweep of its comprehension all sorts and conditions of men; that vision which sees that no society is renewed from the top but that every society is renewed from the bottom. Limit opportunity, restrict the field of originative achievement, and you have cut out the heart and root of all prosperity.

The only thing that can ever make a free country is to keep a free and hopeful heart under every jacket in it. Honest American industry has always thriven, when it has thriven at all, on freedom; it has never thriven on monopoly. It is a great deal better to shift for yourselves than to be taken care of by a great combination of capital. I, for my part, do not want to be taken care of. I would rather starve a free man than be fed a mere thing at the caprice of those who are organizing American industry as they please to organize it. I know, and every man in his heart knows, that the only way to enrich America is to make it possible for any man who has the brains to get into the game. I am not jealous of the size of any business that has *grown* to that size. I am not jealous of any process of growth, no matter how huge the result, provided the result was indeed obtained by the processes of wholesome development, which are the processes of efficiency, of economy, of intelligence, and of invention.

# IX

# BENEVOLENCE, OR JUSTICE?

The doctrine that monopoly is inevitable and that the only course open to the people of the United States is to submit to and regulate it found a champion during the campaign of 1912 in the new party, or branch of the Republican party, founded under the leadership of Mr. Roosevelt, with the conspicuous aid,—I mention him with no satirical intention, but merely to set the facts down accurately,—of Mr. George W. Perkins, organizer of the Steel Trust and the Harvester Trust, and with the support of more than three millions of citizens, many of them among the most patriotic, conscientious and high-minded men and women of the land. The fact that its acceptance of monopoly was a feature of the new party platform from which the attention of the generous and just was diverted by the charm of a social program of great attractiveness to all concerned for the amelioration of the lot of those who suffer wrong and privation, and the further fact that, even so, the platform was repudiated by the majority of the nation, render it no less necessary to reflect on the significance of the confession made for the first time by any party in the country's history. It may be useful, in order to the relief of the minds of many from an error of no small magnitude, to consider now, the heat of a presidential contest being past, exactly what it was that Mr. Roosevelt proposed.

Mr. Roosevelt attached to his platform some very splendid suggestions as to noble enterprises which we ought to undertake for the uplift of the human race; but when I hear an ambitious platform put forth, I am very much more interested in the dynamics of it than in the rhetoric of it. I have a very practical mind, and I want to know who are going to do those things and how they are going to be done. If you have read the trust plank in that platform as often as I have read it, you have found it very long, but very tolerant. It did not anywhere condemn monopoly, except in words; its essential meaning was that the trusts have been bad and must be made to be good. You know that Mr. Roosevelt long ago classified trusts for us as good and bad, and he said that he was afraid only of the bad ones. Now he does not desire that there should be any more bad ones, but proposes that they should all be made good by discipline, directly applied by a commission of executive appointment. All he explicitly complains of is lack of publicity and lack of fairness; not the exercise of power, for throughout that plank the power of the great corporations is accepted as the inevitable consequence of the modern organization of industry. All that it is proposed to do is to take them under control and regulation. The national administration having for sixteen years been virtually under the regulation of the trusts, it would be merely a family matter were the parts reversed and were the other members of the family to exercise the regulation. And the trusts, apparently, which might, in such circumstances, comfortably continue to administer our affairs under the mollifying influences of the federal government, would then, if you please, be the instrumentalities by which all the humanistic, benevolent program of the rest of that interesting platform would be carried out!

I have read and reread that plank, so as to be sure that I get it right. All that it complains of is,—and the complaint is a just one, surely,—that these gentlemen exercise their power in a way that is secret. Therefore, we must have publicity. Sometimes they are arbitrary; therefore they need regulation. Sometimes they do not consult the general interests of the community; therefore they need to be reminded of those general interests by an industrial commission. But at every turn it is the trusts who are to do us good, and not we ourselves.

Again, I absolutely protest against being put into the hands of trustees. Mr. Roosevelt's conception of government is Mr. Taft's conception, that the Presidency of the United States is the presidency of a board of directors. I am willing to admit that if the people of the United States cannot get justice for themselves, then it is high time that they should join the third party and get it from somebody else. The justice proposed is very beautiful; it is very attractive; there were planks in that platform which stir all the sympathies of the heart; they proposed things that we all want to do; but the question is, Who is going to do them? Through whose instrumentality? Are Americans ready to ask the trusts to give us in pity what we ought, in justice, to take?

The third party says that the present system of our industry and trade has come to stay. Mind you, these artificially built up things, these things that can't maintain themselves in the market without monopoly, have come to stay, and the only thing that the government can do, the only thing that the third party proposes should be done, is to set up a commission to regulate them. It accepts them. It says: "We will not undertake, it were futile to undertake, to prevent monopoly, but we will go into an arrangement by which we will make these monopolies kind to you. We will guarantee that they shall be pitiful. We will guarantee that they shall pay the right wages. We will guarantee that they shall do everything kind and public-spirited, which they have never heretofore shown the least inclination to do."

Don't you realize that that is a blind alley? You can't find your way to liberty that way. You can't find your way to social reform through the forces that have made social reform necessary.

The fundamental part of such a program is that the trusts shall be recognized as a permanent part of our economic order, and that the government shall try to make trusts the ministers, the instruments, through which the life of this country shall be justly and happily developed on its industrial side. Now, everything that touches our lives sooner or later goes back to the industries which sustain our lives. I have often reflected that there is a very human order in the petitions in our Lord's prayer. For we pray first of all, "Give us this day our daily bread," knowing that it is useless to pray for spiritual graces on an empty stomach, and that the amount of wages we get, the kind of clothes we wear, the kind of food we can afford to buy, is fundamental to everything else.

Those who administer our physical life, therefore, administer our spiritual life; and if we are going to carry out the fine purpose of that great chorus which supporters of the third party sang almost with religious fervor, then we have got to find out through whom these purposes of humanity are going to be realized. It is a mere enterprise, so far as that part of it is concerned, of making the monopolies philanthropic.

I do not want to live under a philanthropy. I do not want to be taken care of by the government, either directly, or by any instruments through which the government is acting. I want only to have right and justice prevail, so far as I am concerned. Give me right and justice and I will undertake to take care of myself. If you enthrone the trusts as the means of the development of this country under the supervision of the government, then I shall pray the old Spanish proverb, "God save me from my friends, and I'll take care of my enemies." Because I want to be saved from these friends. Observe that I say these friends, for I am ready to admit that a great many men who believe that the development of industry in this country through monopolies is inevitable intend to be the friends of the people. Though they profess to be my friends, they are undertaking a way of friendship which renders it impossible that they should do me the fundamental service that I demand—namely, that I should be free and should have the same opportunities that everybody else has.

For I understand it to be the fundamental proposition of American liberty that we do not desire special privilege, because we know special privilege will never comprehend the general welfare. This is the fundamental, spiritual difference between adherents of the party now about to take charge of the government and those who have been in charge of it in recent years. They are so indoctrinated with the idea that only the big business interests of this country understand the United States and can make it prosperous that they cannot divorce their thoughts from that obsession. They have put the government into the hands of trustees, and Mr. Taft and Mr. Roosevelt were the rival candidates to preside over the board of trustees. They were candidates to serve the people, no doubt, to the best of their ability, but it was not their idea to serve them directly; they proposed to serve them indirectly through the enormous forces already set up, which are so great that there is almost an open question whether the government of the United States with the people back of it is strong enough to overcome and rule them.

---

Shall we try to get the grip of monopoly away from our lives, or shall we not? Shall we withhold our hand and say monopoly is inevitable, that all that we can do is to regulate it? Shall we say that all that we can do is to put government in competition with monopoly and try its strength against it? Shall we admit that the creature of our own hands is stronger than we are? We have been dreading all along the time when the combined power of high finance would be greater than the power of the government. Have we come to a time when the President of the United States or any man who wishes to be the President must doff his cap in the presence of this high finance, and say, "You are our inevitable master, but we will see how we can make the best of it?"

We are at the parting of the ways. We have, not one or two or three, but many, established and formidable monopolies in the United States. We have, not one or two, but many, fields of endeavor into which it is difficult, if not impossible, for the independent man to enter. We have restricted credit, we have restricted opportunity, we have controlled development, and we have come to be one of the worst ruled, one of the most completely controlled and dominated, governments in the civilized world—no longer a government by free opinion, no longer a government by conviction and the vote of the majority, but a government by the opinion and the duress of small groups of dominant men.

If the government is to tell big business men how to run their business, then don't you see that big business men have to get closer to the government even than they are now? Don't you see that they must capture the government, in order not to be restrained too much by it? Must capture the government? They have already captured it. Are you going to invite those inside to stay inside? They don't have to get there. They are there. Are you going to own your own premises, or are you not? That is your choice. Are you going to say: "You didn't get into the house the right way, but you are in there, God bless you; we will stand out here in the cold and you can hand us out something once in a while?"

At the least, under the plan I am opposing, there will be an avowed partnership between the government and the trusts. I take it that the firm will be ostensibly controlled by the senior member. For I take it that the government of the United States is at least the senior member, though the younger member has all along been running the business. But when all the momentum, when all the energy, when a great deal of the genius, as so often happens in partnerships the world over, is with the junior partner, I don't think that the superintendence of the senior partner is going to amount to very much. And I don't believe that benevolence can be read into the hearts of the trusts by the superintendence and suggestions of the federal government; because the government has never within my recollection had its suggestions accepted by the trusts. On the contrary, the suggestions of the trusts have been accepted by the government.

There is no hope to be seen for the people of the United States until the partnership is dissolved. And the business of the party now entrusted with power is going to be to dissolve it.

---

Those who supported the third party supported, I believe, a program perfectly agreeable to the monopolies. How those who have been fighting monopoly through all their career can reconcile the continuation of the battle under the banner of the very men they have been fighting, I cannot imagine. I challenge the program in its fundamentals as not a progressive program at all. Why did Mr. Gary suggest this very method when he was at the head of the Steel Trust? Why is this very method commended here, there, and everywhere by the men who are interested in the maintenance of the present economic system of the United States? Why do the men who do not wish to be disturbed urge the adoption of this program? The rest of the program is very handsome; there is beating in it a great pulse of sympathy for the human race. But I do not want the sympathy of the trusts for the human race. I do not want their condescending assistance.

And I warn every progressive Republican that by lending his assistance to this program he is playing false to the very cause in which he had enlisted. That cause was a battle against monopoly, against control, against the concentration of power in our economic development, against all those things that interfere with absolutely free enterprise. I believe that some day these gentlemen will wake up and realize that they have misplaced their trust, not in an individual, it may be, but in a program which is fatal to the things we hold dearest.

If there is any meaning in the things I have been urging, it is this: that the incubus that lies upon this country is the present monopolistic organization of our industrial life. That is the thing which certain Republicans became "insurgents" in order to throw off. And yet some of them allowed themselves to be so misled as to go into the camp of the third party in order to remove what the third party proposed to legalize. My point is that this is a method conceived from the point of view of the very men who are to be controlled, and that this is just the wrong point of view from which to conceive it.

I said not long ago that Mr. Roosevelt was promoting a plan for the control of monopoly which was supported by the United States Steel Corporation. Mr. Roosevelt denied that he was being supported by more than one member of that corporation. He was thinking of money. I was thinking of ideas. I did not say that he was getting money from these gentlemen; it was a matter of indifference to me where he got his money; but it was a matter of a great deal of difference to me where he got his ideas. He got his idea with regard to the regulation of monopoly from the gentlemen who form the United States Steel Corporation. I am perfectly ready to admit that the gentlemen who control the United States Steel Corporation have a perfect right to entertain their own ideas about this and to urge them upon the people of the United States; but I want to say that their ideas are not my ideas; and I am perfectly certain that they would not promote any idea which interfered with their monopoly. Inasmuch, therefore, as I hope and intend to interfere with monopoly just as much as possible, I cannot subscribe to arrangements by which they know that it will not be disturbed.

The Roosevelt plan is that there shall be an industrial commission charged with the supervision of the great monopolistic combinations which have been formed under the protection of the tariff, and that the government of the United States shall see to it that these gentlemen who have conquered labor shall be kind to labor. I find, then, the proposition to be this: That there shall be two masters, the great corporation, and over it the government of the United States; and I ask who is going to be master of the government of the United States? It has a master now,—those who in combination control these monopolies. And if the government controlled by the monopolies in its turn controls the monopolies, the partnership is finally consummated.

I don't care how benevolent the master is going to be, I will not live under a master. That is not what America was created for. America was created in order that every man should have the same chance as every other man to exercise mastery over his own fortunes. What I want to do is analogous to what the authorities of the city of Glasgow did with tenement houses. I want to light and patrol the corridors of these great organizations in order to see that nobody who tries to traverse them is waylaid and maltreated. If you will but hold off the adversaries, if you will but see to it that the weak are protected, I will venture a wager with you that there are some men in the United States, now weak, economically weak, who have brains enough to compete with these gentlemen and who will presently come into the market and put these gentlemen on their mettle. And the minute they come into the market there will be a bigger market for labor and a different wage scale for labor.

Because it is susceptible of convincing proof that the high-paid labor of America,—where it is high paid,—is cheaper than the low-paid labor of the continent of Europe. Do you know that about ninety per cent. of those who are employed in labor in this country are not employed in the "protected" industries, and that their wages are almost without exception higher than the wages of those who are employed in the "protected" industries? There is no corner on carpenters, there is no corner on bricklayers, there is no corner on scores of individual classes of skilled laborers; but there is a corner on the poolers in the furnaces, there is a corner on the men who dive down into the mines; they are in the grip of a controlling power which determines the market rates of wages in the United States. Only where labor is free is labor highly paid in America.

When I am fighting monopolistic control, therefore, I am fighting for the liberty of every man in America, and I am fighting for the liberty of American industry.

It is significant that the spokesman for the plan of adopting monopoly declares his devoted adherence to the principle of "protection." Only those duties which are manifestly too high even to serve the interests of those who are directly "protected" ought in his view to be lowered. He declares that he is not troubled by the fact that a very large amount of money is taken out of the pocket of the general taxpayer and put into the pocket of particular classes of "protected" manufacturers, but that his concern is that so little of this money gets into the pocket of the laboring man and so large a proportion of it into the pockets of the employers. I have searched his program very thoroughly for an indication of what he expects to do in order to see to it that a larger proportion of this "prize" money gets into the pay envelope, and have found none. Mr. Roosevelt, in one of his speeches, proposed that manufacturers who did not share their profits liberally enough with their workmen should be penalized by a sharp cut in the "protection" afforded them; but the platform, so far as I could see, proposed nothing.

Moreover, under the system proposed, most employers,—at any rate, practically all of the most powerful of them,—would be, to all intents and purposes, wards and protégés of the government which is the master of us all; for no part of this program can be discussed intelligently without remembering that monopoly, as handled by it, is not to be prevented, but accepted. It is to be accepted and regulated. All attempt to resist it is to be given up. It is to be accepted as inevitable. The government is to set up a commission whose duty it will be, not to check or defeat it, but merely to regulate it under rules which it is itself to frame and develop. So that the chief employers will have this tremendous authority behind them: what they do, they will have the license of the federal government to do.

And it is worth the while of the workingmen of the country to recall what the attitude toward organized labor has been of these masters of consolidated industries whom it is proposed that the federal government should take under its patronage as well as under its control. They have been the stoutest and most successful opponents of organized labor, and they have tried to undermine it in a great many ways. Some of the ways they have adopted have worn the guise of philanthropy and good-will, and have no doubt been used, for all I know, in perfect good faith. Here and there they have set up systems of profit sharing, of compensation for injuries, and of bonuses, and even pensions; but every one of these plans has merely bound their workingmen more tightly to themselves. Rights under these various arrangements are not legal rights. They are merely privileges which employees enjoy only so long as they remain in the employment and observe the rules of the great industries for which they work. If they refuse to be weaned away from their independence they cannot continue to enjoy the benefits extended to them.

---

When you have thought the whole thing out, therefore, you will find that the program of the new party legalizes monopolies and systematically subordinates workingmen to them and to plans made by the government both with regard to employment and with regard to wages. Take the thing as a whole, and it looks strangely like economic mastery over the very lives and fortunes of those who do the daily work of the nation; and all this under the overwhelming power and sovereignty of the national government. What most of us are fighting for is to break up this very partnership between big business and the government. We call upon all intelligent men to bear witness that if this plan were consummated, the great employers and capitalists of the country would be under a more overpowering temptation than ever to take control of the government and keep it subservient to their purpose.

What a prize it would be to capture! How unassailable would be the majesty and the tyranny of monopoly if it could thus get sanction of law and the authority of government! By what means, except open revolt, could we ever break the crust of our life again and become free men, breathing an air of our own, living lives that we wrought out for ourselves?

You cannot use monopoly in order to serve a free people. You cannot use great combinations of capital to be pitiful and righteous when the consciences of great bodies of men are enlisted, not in the promotion of special privilege, but in the realization of human rights. When I read those beautiful portions of the program of the third party devoted to the uplift of mankind and see noble men and women attaching themselves to that party in the hope that regulated monopoly may realize these dreams of humanity, I wonder whether they have really studied the instruments through which they are going to do these things. The man who is leading the third party has not changed his point of view since he was President of the United States. I am not asking him to change it. I am not saying that he has not a perfect right to retain it. But I do say that it is not surprising that a man who had the point of view with regard to the government of this country which he had when he was President was not chosen as President again, and allowed to patent the present processes of industry and personally direct them how to treat the people of the United States.

There has been a history of the human race, you know, and a history of government; it is recorded; and the kind of thing proposed has been tried again and again and has always led to the same result. History is strewn all along its course with the wrecks of governments that tried to be humane, tried to carry out humane programs through the instrumentality of those who controlled the material fortunes of the rest of their fellow-citizens.

I do not trust any promises of a change of temper on the part of monopoly. Monopoly never was conceived in the temper of tolerance. Monopoly never was conceived with the purpose of general development. It was conceived with the purpose of special advantage. Has monopoly been very benevolent to its employees? Have the trusts had a soft heart for the working people of America? Have you found trusts that cared whether women were sapped of their vitality or not? Have you found trusts who are very scrupulous about using children in their tender years? Have you found trusts that were keen to protect the lungs and the health and the freedom of their employees? Have you found trusts that thought as much of their men as they did of their machinery? Then who is going to convert these men into the chief instruments of justice and benevolence?

If you will point me to the least promise of disinterestedness on the part of the masters of our lives, then I will conceive you some ray of hope; but only upon this hypothesis, only upon this conjecture: that the history of the world is going to be reversed, and that the men who have the power to oppress us will be kind to us, and will promote our interests, whether our interests jump with theirs or not.

After you have made the partnership between monopoly and your government permanent, then I invite all the philanthropists in the United States to come and sit on the stage and go through the motions of finding out how they are going to get philanthropy out of their masters.

I do not want to see the special interests of the United States take care of the workingmen, women, and children. I want to see justice, righteousness, fairness and humanity displayed in all the laws of the United States, and I do not want any power to intervene between the people and their government. Justice is what we want, not patronage and condescension and pitiful helpfulness. The trusts are our masters now, but I for one do not care to live in a country called free even under kind masters. I prefer to live under no masters at all.

---

I agree that as a nation we are now about to undertake what may be regarded as the most difficult part of our governmental enterprises. We have gone along so far without very much assistance from our government. We have felt, and felt more and more in recent months, that the American people were at a certain disadvantage as compared with the people of other countries, because of what the governments of other countries were doing for them and our government omitting to do for us.

It is perfectly clear to every man who has any vision of the immediate future, who can forecast any part of it from the indications of the present, that we are just upon the threshold of a time when the systematic life of this country will be sustained, or at least supplemented, at every point by governmental activity. And we have now to determine what kind of governmental activity it shall be; whether, in the first place, it shall be direct from the government itself, or whether it shall be indirect, through instrumentalities which have already constituted themselves and which stand ready to supersede the government.

I believe that the time has come when the governments of this country, both state and national, have to set the stage, and set it very minutely and carefully, for the doing of justice to men in every relationship of life. It has been free and easy with us so far; it has been go as you please; it has been every man look out for himself; and we have continued to assume, up to this year when every man is dealing, not with another man, in most cases, but with a body of men whom he has not seen, that the relationships of property are the same that they always were. We have great tasks before us, and we must enter on them as befits men charged with the responsibility of shaping a new era.

We have a great program of governmental assistance ahead of us in the co-operative life of the nation; but we dare not enter upon that program until we have freed the government. That is the point. Benevolence never developed a man or a nation. We do not want a benevolent government. We want a free and a just government. Every one of the great schemes of social uplift which are now so much debated by noble people amongst us is based, when rightly conceived, upon justice, not upon benevolence. It is based upon the right of men to breathe pure air, to live; upon the right of women to bear children, and not to be overburdened so that disease and breakdown will come upon them; upon the right of children to thrive and grow up and be strong; upon all these fundamental things which appeal, indeed, to our hearts, but which our minds perceive to be part of the fundamental justice of life.

Politics differs from philanthropy in this: that in philanthropy we sometimes do things through pity merely, while in politics we act always, if we are righteous men, on grounds of justice and large expediency for men in the mass. Sometimes in our pitiful sympathy with our fellow-men we must do things that are more than just. We must forgive men. We must help men who have gone wrong. We must sometimes help men who have gone criminally wrong. But the law does not forgive. It is its duty to equalize conditions, to make the path of right the path of safety and advantage, to see that every man has a fair chance to live and to serve himself, to see that injustice and wrong are not wrought upon any.

We ought not to permit passion to enter into our thoughts or our hearts in this great matter; we ought not to allow ourselves to be governed by resentment or any kind of evil feeling, but we ought, nevertheless, to realize the seriousness of our situation. That seriousness consists, singularly enough, not in the malevolence of the men who preside over our industrial life, but in their genius and in their honest thinking. These men believe that the prosperity of the United States is not safe unless it is in their keeping. If they were dishonest, we might put them out of business by law; since most of them are honest, we can put them out of business only by making it impossible for them to realize their genuine convictions. I am not afraid of a knave. I am not afraid of a rascal. I am afraid of a strong man who is wrong, and whose wrong thinking can be impressed upon other persons by his own force of character and force of speech. If God had only arranged it that all the men who are wrong were rascals, we could put them out of business very easily, because they would give themselves away sooner or later; but God has made our task heavier than that,—he has made some good men who think wrong. We cannot fight them because they are bad, but because they are wrong. We must overcome them by a better force, the genial, the splendid, the permanent force of a better reason.

The reason that America was set up was that she might be different from all the nations of the world in this: that the strong could not put the weak to the wall, that the strong could not prevent the weak from entering the race. America stands for opportunity. America stands for a free field and no favor. America stands for a government responsive to the interests of all. And until America recovers those ideals in practice, she will not have the right to hold her head high again amidst the nations as she used to hold it.

---

It is like coming out of a stifling cellar into the open where we can breathe again and see the free spaces of the heavens to turn away from such a doleful program of submission and dependence toward the other plan, the confident purpose for which the people have given their mandate. Our purpose is the restoration of freedom. We purpose to prevent private monopoly by law, to see to it that the methods by which monopolies have been built up are legally made impossible. We design that the limitations on private enterprise shall be removed, so that the next generation of youngsters, as they come along, will not have to become protégés of benevolent trusts, but will be free to go about making their own lives what they will; so that we shall taste again the full cup, not of charity, but of liberty,—the only wine that ever refreshed and renewed the spirit of a people.

X

# THE WAY TO RESUME IS TO RESUME

One of the wonderful things about America, to my mind, is this: that for more than a generation it has allowed itself to be governed by persons who were not invited to govern it. A singular thing about the people of the United States is their almost infinite patience, their willingness to stand quietly by and see things done which they have voted against and do not want done, and yet never lay the hand of disorder upon any arrangement of government.

There is hardly a part of the United States where men are not aware that secret private purposes and interests have been running the government. They have been running it through the agency of those interesting persons whom we call political "bosses." A boss is not so much a politician as the business agent in politics of the special interests. The boss is not a partisan; he is quite above politics! He has an understanding with the boss of the other party, so that, whether it is heads or tails, we lose. The two receive contributions from the same sources, and they spend those contributions for the same purposes.

Bosses are men who have worked their way by secret methods to the place of power they occupy; men who were never elected to anything; men who were not asked by the people to conduct their government, and who are very much more powerful than if you had asked them, so long as you leave them where they are, behind closed doors, in secret conference. They are not politicians; they have no policies,—except concealed policies of private aggrandizement. A boss isn't a leader of a party. Parties do not meet in back rooms; parties do not make arrangements which do not get into the newspapers. Parties, if you reckon them by voting strength, are great masses of men who, because they can't vote any other ticket, vote the ticket that was prepared for them by the aforesaid arrangement in the aforesaid back room in accordance with the aforesaid understanding. A boss is the manipulator of a "machine." A "machine" is that part of a political organization which has been taken out of the hands of the rank and file of the party, captured by half a dozen men. It is the part that has ceased to be political and has become an agency for the purposes of unscrupulous business.

Do not lay up the sins of this kind of business to political organizations. Organization is legitimate, is necessary, is even distinguished, when it lends itself to the carrying out of great causes. Only the man who uses organization to promote private purposes is a boss. Always distinguish between a political leader and a boss. I honor the man who makes the organization of a great party strong and thorough, in order to use it for public service. But he is not a boss. A boss is a man who uses this splendid, open force for secret purposes.

One of the worst features of the boss system is this fact, that it works secretly. I would a great deal rather live under a king whom I should at least know, than under a boss whom I don't know. A boss is a much more formidable master than a king, because a king is an obvious master, whereas the hands of the boss are always where you least expect them to be.

When I was in Oregon, not many months ago, I had some very interesting conversations with Mr. U'Ren, who is the father of what is called the Oregon System, a system by which he has put bosses out of business. He is a member of a group of public-spirited men who, whenever they cannot get what they want through the legislature, draw up a bill and submit it to the people, by means of the initiative, and generally get what they want. The day I arrived in Portland, a morning paper happened to say, very ironically, that there were two legislatures in Oregon, one at Salem, the state capital, and the other going around under the hat of Mr. U'Ren. I could not resist the temptation of saying, when I spoke that evening, that, while I was the last man to suggest that power should be concentrated in any single individual or group of individuals, I would, nevertheless, after my experience in New Jersey, rather have a legislature that went around under the hat of somebody in particular whom I knew I could find than a legislature that went around under God knows who's hat; because then you could at least put your finger on your governing force; you would know where to find it.

Why do we continue to permit these things? Isn't it about time that we grew up and took charge of our own affairs? I am tired of being under age in politics. I don't want to be associated with anybody except those who are politically over twenty-one. I don't wish to sit down and let any man take care of me without my having at least a voice in it; and if he doesn't listen to my advice, I am going to make it as unpleasant for him as I can. Not because my advice is necessarily good, but because no government is good in which every man doesn't insist upon his advice being heard, at least, whether it is heeded or not.

Some persons have said that representative government has proved too indirect and clumsy an instrument, and has broken down as a means of popular control. Others, looking a little deeper, have said that it was not representative government that had broken down, but the effort to get it. They have pointed out that, with our present methods of machine nomination and our present methods of election, which give us nothing more than a choice between one set of machine nominees and another, we do not get representative government at all,—at least not government representative of the people, but merely government representative of political managers who serve their own interests and the interests of those with whom they find it profitable to establish partnerships.

Obviously, this is something that goes to the root of the whole matter. Back of all reform lies the method of getting it. Back of the question, What do you want, lies the question,—the fundamental question of all government, —How are you going to get it? How are you going to get public servants who will obtain it for you? How are you going to get genuine representatives who will serve your interests, and not their own or the interests of some special group or body of your fellow-citizens whose power is of the few and not of the many? These are the queries which have drawn the attention of the whole country to the subject of the direct primary, the direct choice of their officials by the people, without the intervention of the nominating machine; to the subject of the direct election of United States Senators; and to the question of the initiative, referendum, and recall.

---

The critical moment in the choosing of officials is that of their nomination more often than that of their election. When two party organizations, nominally opposing each other but actually working in perfect understanding and co-operation, see to it that both tickets have the same kind of men on them, it is Tweedledum or Tweedledee, so far as the people are concerned; the political managers have us coming and going. We may delude ourselves with the pleasing belief that we are electing our own officials, but of course the fact is we are merely making an indifferent and ineffectual choice between two sets of men named by interests which are not ours.

So that what we establish the direct primary for is this: to break up the inside and selfish determination of the question who shall be elected to conduct the government and make the laws of our commonwealths and our nation. Everywhere the impression is growing stronger that there can be no means of dominating those who have dominated us except by taking this process of the original selection of nominees into our own hands. Does that upset any ancient foundations? Is it not the most natural and simple thing in the world? You say that it does not always work; that the people are too busy or too lazy to bother about voting at primary elections? True, sometimes the people of a state or a community do let a direct primary go by without asserting their authority as against the bosses. The electorate of the United States is occasionally like the god Baal: it is sometimes on a journey or it is sometimes asleep; but when it does awake, it does not resemble the god Baal in the slightest degree. It is a great self-possessed power which effectually takes control of its own affairs. I am willing to wait. I am among those who believe so firmly in the essential doctrines of democracy that I am willing to wait on the convenience of this great sovereign, provided I know that he has got the instrument to dominate whenever he chooses to grasp it.

Then there is another thing that the conservative people are concerned about: the direct election of United States Senators. I have seen some thoughtful men discuss that with a sort of shiver, as if to disturb the original constitution of the United States Senate was to do something touched with impiety, touched with irreverence for the Constitution itself. But the first thing necessary to reverence for the United States Senate is respect for United States Senators. I am not one of those who condemn the United States Senate as a body; for, no matter what has happened there, no matter how questionable the practices or how corrupt the influences which have filled some of the seats in that high body, it must in fairness be said that the majority in it has all the years through been untouched by stain, and that there has always been there a sufficient number of men of integrity to vindicate the self-respect and the hopefulness of America with regard to her institutions.

But you need not be told, and it would be painful to repeat to you, how seats have been bought in the Senate; and you know that a little group of Senators holding the balance of power has again and again been able to defeat programs of reform upon which the whole country had set its heart; and that whenever you analyzed the power that was behind those little groups you have found that it was not the power of public opinion, but some private influence, hardly to be discerned by superficial scrutiny, that had put those men there to do that thing.

Now, returning to the original principles upon which we profess to stand, have the people of the United States not the right to see to it that every seat in the Senate represents the unbought United States of America? Does the direct election of Senators touch anything except the private control of seats in the Senate? We remember another thing: that we have not been without our suspicions concerning some of the legislatures which elect Senators. Some of the suspicions which we entertained in New Jersey about them turned out to be founded upon very solid facts indeed. Until two years ago New Jersey had not in half a generation been represented in the United States Senate by the men who would have been chosen if the process of selecting them had been free and based upon the popular will.

We are not to deceive ourselves by putting our heads into the sand and saying, "Everything is all right." Mr. Gladstone declared that the American Constitution was the most perfect instrument ever devised by the brain of man. We have been praised all over the world for our singular genius for setting up successful institutions, but a very thoughtful Englishman, and a very witty one, said a very instructive thing about that: he said that to show that the American Constitution had worked well was no proof that it is an excellent constitution, because Americans could run any constitution,—a compliment which we laid like sweet unction to our soul; and yet a criticism which ought to set us thinking.

While it is true that when American forces are awake they can conduct American processes without serious departure from the ideals of the Constitution, it is nevertheless true that we have had many shameful instances of practices which we can absolutely remove by the direct election of Senators by the people themselves. And therefore I, for one, will not allow any man who knows his history to say to me that I am acting inconsistently with either the spirit or the essential form of the American government in advocating the direct election of United States Senators.

Take another matter. Take the matter of the initiative and referendum, and the recall. There are communities, there are states in the Union, in which I am quite ready to admit that it is perhaps premature, that perhaps it will never be necessary, to discuss these measures. But I want to call your attention to the fact that they have been adopted to the general satisfaction in a number of states where the electorate had become convinced that they did not have representative government.

Why do you suppose that in the United States, the place in all the world where the people were invited to control their own government, we should set up such an agitation as that for the initiative and referendum and the recall. When did this thing begin? I have been receiving circulars and documents from little societies of men all over the United States with regard to these matters, for the last twenty-five years. But the circulars for a long time kindled no fire. Men felt that they had representative government and they were content. But about ten or fifteen years ago the fire began to burn,—and it has been sweeping over wider and wider areas of the country, because of the growing consciousness that something intervenes between the people and the government, and that there must be some arm direct enough and strong enough to thrust aside the something that comes in the way.

I believe that we are upon the eve of recovering some of the most important prerogatives of a free people, and that the initiative and referendum are playing a great part in that recovery. I met a man the other day who thought that the referendum was some kind of an animal, because it had a Latin name; and there are still people in this country who have to have it explained to them. But most of us know and are deeply interested. Why? Because we have felt that in too many instances our government did not represent us, and we have said: "We have got to have a key to the door of our own house. The initiative and referendum and the recall afford such a key to our own premises. If the people inside the house will run the place as we want it run, they may stay inside and we will keep the latchkeys in our pockets. If they do not, we shall have to re-enter upon possession."

Let no man be deceived by the cry that somebody is proposing to substitute direct legislation by the people, or the direct reference of laws passed in the legislature, to the vote of the people, for representative government. The advocates of these reforms have always declared, and declared in unmistakable terms, that they were intending to recover representative government, not supersede it; that the initiative and referendum would find no use in places where legislatures were really representative of the people whom they were elected to serve. The initiative is a means of seeing to it that measures which the people want shall be passed,—when legislatures defy or ignore public opinion. The referendum is a means of seeing to it that the unrepresentative measures which they do not want shall not be placed upon the statute book.

When you come to the recall, the principle is that if an administrative officer,—for we will begin with the administrative officer,—is corrupt or so unwise as to be doing things that are likely to lead to all sorts of mischief, it will be possible by a deliberate process prescribed by the law to get rid of that officer before the end of his term. You must admit that it is a little inconvenient sometimes to have what has been called an astronomical system of government, in which you can't change anything until there has been a certain number of revolutions of the seasons. In many of our oldest states the ordinary administrative term is a single year. The people of those states have not been willing to trust an official out of their sight more than twelve months. Elections there are a sort of continuous performance, based on the idea of the constant touch of the hand of the people on their own affairs. That is exactly the principle of the recall. I don't see how any man grounded in the traditions of American affairs can find any valid objection to the recall of administrative officers. The meaning of the recall is merely this,—not that we should have unstable government, not that officials should not know how long their power might last,—but that we might have government exercised by officials who know whence their power came and that if they yield to private influences they will presently be displaced by public influences.

You will of course understand that, both in the case of the initiative and referendum and in that of the recall, the very existence of these powers, the very possibilities which they imply, are half,—indeed, much more than half, —the battle. They rarely need to be actually exercised. The fact that the people may initiate keeps the members of the legislature awake to the necessity of initiating themselves; the fact that the people have the right to demand the submission of a legislative measure to popular vote renders the members of the legislature wary of bills that would not pass the people; the very possibility of being recalled puts the official on his best behavior.

It is another matter when we come to the judiciary. I myself have never been in favor of the recall of judges. Not because some judges have not deserved to be recalled. That isn't the point. The point is that the recall of judges is treating the symptom instead of the disease. The disease lies deeper, and sometimes it is very virulent and very dangerous. There have been courts in the United States which were controlled by private interests. There have been supreme courts in our states before which plain men could not get justice. There have been corrupt judges; there have been controlled judges; there have been judges who acted as other men's servants and not as the servants of the public. Ah, there are some shameful chapters in the story! The judicial process is the ultimate safeguard of the things that we must hold stable in this country. But suppose that that safeguard is corrupted; suppose that it does not guard my interests and yours, but guards merely the interests of a very small group of individuals; and, whenever your interest clashes with theirs, yours will have to give way, though you represent ninety per cent. of the citizens, and they only ten per cent. Then where is your safeguard?

The just thought of the people must control the judiciary, as it controls every other instrument of government. But there are ways and ways of controlling it. If,—mark you, I say *if*,—at one time the Southern Pacific Railroad owned the supreme court of the State of California, would you remedy that situation by recalling the judges of the court? What good would that do, so long as the Southern Pacific Railroad could substitute others for them? You would not be cutting deep enough. Where you want to go is to the process by which those judges were selected. And when you get there, you will reach the moral of the whole of this discussion, because the moral of it all is that the people of the United States have suspected, until their suspicions have been justified by all sorts of substantial and unanswerable evidence, that, in place after place, at turning-points in the history of this country, we have been controlled by private understandings and not by the public interest; and that influences which were improper, if not corrupt, have determined everything from the making of laws to the administration of justice. The disease lies in the region where these men get their nominations; and if you can recover for the people the *selecting* of judges, you will not have to trouble about their recall. Selection is of more radical consequence than election.

---

I am aware that those who advocate these measures which we have been discussing are denounced as dangerous radicals. I am particularly interested to observe that the men who cry out most loudly against what they call radicalism are the men who find that their private game in politics is being spoiled. Who are the arch-conservatives nowadays? Who are the men who utter the most fervid praise of the Constitution of the United States and the constitutions of the states? They are the gentlemen who used to get behind those documents to play hide-and-seek with the people whom they pretended to serve. They are the men who entrenched themselves in the laws which they misinterpreted and misused. If now they are afraid that "radicalism" will sweep them away,—and I believe it will,—they have only themselves to thank.

Yet how absurd is the charge that we who are demanding that our government be made representative of the people and responsive to their demands,—how fictitious and hypocritical is the charge that we are attacking the fundamental principles of republican institutions! These very men who hysterically profess their alarm would declaim loudly enough on the Fourth of July of the Declaration of Independence; they would go on and talk of those splendid utterances in our earliest state constitutions, which have been copied in all our later ones, taken from the Petition of Rights, or the Declaration of Rights, those great fundamental documents of the struggle for liberty in England; and yet in these very documents we read such uncompromising statements as this: that, when at any time the people of a commonwealth find that their government is not suitable to the circumstances of their lives or the promotion of their liberties, it is their privilege to alter it at their pleasure, and alter it in any degree. That is the foundation, that is the very central doctrine, that is the ground principle, of American institutions.

I want you to read a passage from the Virginia Bill of Rights, that immortal document which has been a model for declarations of liberty throughout the rest of the continent:

> That all power is vested in, and consequently derived from, the people; that magistrates are their trustees and servants, and at all times amenable to them.
>
> That government is, or ought to be, instituted for the common benefit, protection, and security of the people, nation, or community; of all the various modes and forms of government, that is the best which is capable of producing the greatest degree of happiness and safety, and is most effectually secured against the danger of mal-administration; and that, when any government shall be found inadequate or contrary to these purposes, a majority of the community bath an indubitable, inalienable, and indefeasible right to reform, alter, or abolish it, in such manner as shall be judged most conducive to the public weal.

I have heard that read a score of times on the Fourth of July, but I never heard it read where actual measures were being debated. No man who understands the principles upon which this Republic was founded has the slightest dread of the gentle,—though very effective,—measures by which the people are again resuming control of their own affairs.

---

Nor need any lover of liberty be anxious concerning the outcome of the struggle upon which we are now embarked. The victory is certain, and the battle is not going to be an especially sanguinary one. It is hardly going to be worth the name of a battle. Let me tell the story of the emancipation of one State,—New Jersey:

It has surprised the people of the United States to find New Jersey at the front in enterprises of reform. I, who have lived in New Jersey the greater part of my mature life, know that there is no state in the Union which, so far as the hearts and intelligence of its people are concerned, has more earnestly desired reform than has New Jersey. There are men who have been prominent in the affairs of the State who again and again advocated with all the earnestness that was in them the things that we have at last been able to do. There are men in New Jersey who have spent some of the best energies of their lives in trying to win elections in order to get the support of the citizens of New Jersey for programs of reform.

The people had voted for such things very often before the autumn of 1910, but the interesting thing is that nothing had happened. They were demanding the benefit of remedial measures such as had been passed in every progressive state of the Union, measures which had proved not only that they did not upset the life of the communities to which they were applied but that they quickened every force and bettered every condition in those communities. But the people of New Jersey could not get them, and there had come upon them a certain pessimistic despair. I used to meet men who shrugged their shoulders and said: "What difference does it make how we vote? Nothing ever results from our votes." The force that is behind the new party that has recently been formed, the so-called "Progressive Party," is a force of discontent with the old parties of the United States. It is the feeling that men have gone into blind alleys often enough, and that somehow there must be found an open road through which men may pass to some purpose.

In the year 1910 there came a day when the people of New Jersey took heart to believe that something could be accomplished. I had no merit as a candidate for Governor, except that I said what I really thought, and the compliment that the people paid me was in believing that I meant what I said. Unless they had believed in the Governor whom they then elected, unless they had trusted him deeply and altogether, he could have done absolutely nothing. The force of the public men of a nation lies in the faith and the backing of the people of the country, rather than in any gifts of their own. In proportion as you trust them, in proportion as you back them up, in proportion as you lend them your strength, are they strong. The things that have happened in New Jersey since 1910 have happened because the seed was planted in this fine fertile soil of confidence, of trust, of renewed hope.

The moment the forces in New Jersey that had resisted reform realized that the people were backing new men who meant what they had said, they realized that they dare not resist them. It was not the personal force of the new officials; it was the moral strength of their backing that accomplished the extraordinary result.

And what was accomplished? Mere justice to classes that had not been treated justly before.

Every schoolboy in the State of New Jersey, if he cared to look into the matter, could comprehend the fact that the laws applying to laboring-men with respect of compensation when they were hurt in their various employments had originated at a time when society was organized very differently from the way in which it is organized now, and that because the law had not been changed, the courts were obliged to go blindly on administering laws which were cruelly unsuitable to existing conditions, so that it was practically impossible for the workingmen of New Jersey to get justice from the courts; the legislature of the commonwealth had not come to their assistance with the necessary legislation. Nobody seriously debated the circumstances; everybody knew that the law was antiquated and impossible; everybody knew that justice waited to be done. Very well, then, why wasn't it done?

There was another thing that we wanted to do: We wanted to regulate our public service corporations so that we could get the proper service from them, and on reasonable terms. That had been done elsewhere, and where it had been done it had proved just as much for the benefit of the corporations themselves as for the benefit of the people. Of course it was somewhat difficult to convince the corporations. It happened that one of the men who knew the least about the subject was the president of the Public Service Corporation of New Jersey. I have heard speeches from that gentleman that exhibited a total lack of acquaintance with the circumstances of our times. I have never known ignorance so complete in its detail; and, being a man of force and ignorance, he naturally set all his energy to resist the things that he did not comprehend.

I am not interested in questioning the motives of men in such positions. I am only sorry that they don't know more. If they would only join the procession they would find themselves benefited by the healthful exercise, which, for one thing, would renew within them the capacity to learn which I hope they possessed when they were younger. We were not trying to do anything novel in New Jersey in regulating the Public Service Corporation; we were simply trying to adopt there a tested measure of public justice. We adopted it. Has anybody gone bankrupt since? Does anybody now doubt that it was just as much for the benefit of the Public Service Corporation as for the people of the State?

Then there was another thing that we modestly desired: We wanted fair elections; we did not want candidates to buy themselves into office. That seemed reasonable. So we adopted a law, unique in one particular, namely: that if you bought an office, you didn't get it. I admit that that is contrary to all commercial principles, but I think it is pretty good political doctrine. It is all very well to put a man in jail for buying an office, but it is very much better, besides putting him in jail, to show him that if he has paid out a single dollar for that office, he does not get it, though a huge majority voted for him. We reversed the laws of trade; when you buy something in politics in New Jersey, you do not get it. It seemed to us that that was the best way to discourage improper political argument. If your money does not produce the goods, then you are not tempted to spend your money.

We adopted a Corrupt Practices Act, the reasonable foundation of which no man could question, and an Election Act, which every man predicted was not going to work, but which did work,—to the emancipation of the voters of New Jersey.

All these things are now commonplaces with us. We like the laws that we have passed, and no man ventures to suggest any material change in them. Why didn't we get them long ago? What hindered us? Why, because we had a closed government; not an open government. It did not belong to us. It was managed by little groups of men whose names we knew, but whom somehow we didn't seem able to dislodge. When we elected men pledged to dislodge them, they only went into partnership with them. Apparently what was necessary was to call in an amateur who knew so little about the game that he supposed that he was expected to do what he had promised to do.

There are gentlemen who have criticised the Governor of New Jersey because he did not do certain things,—for instance, bring a lot of indictments. The Governor of New Jersey does not think it necessary to defend himself; but he would like to call attention to a very interesting thing that happened in his State: When the people had taken over control of the government, a curious change was wrought in the souls of a great many men; a sudden moral awakening took place, and we simply could not find culprits against whom to bring indictments; it was like a Sunday school, the way they obeyed the laws.

---

So I say, there is nothing very difficult about resuming our own government. There is nothing to appall us when we make up our minds to set about the task. "The way to resume is to resume," said Horace Greeley, once, when the country was frightened at a prospect which turned out to be not in the least frightful; it was at the moment of the resumption of specie payments for Treasury notes. The Treasury simply resumed,—there was not a ripple of danger or excitement when the day of resumption came around.

It will be precisely so when the people resume control of their own government. The men who conduct the political machines are a small fraction of the party they pretend to represent, and the men who exercise corrupt influences upon them are only a small fraction of the business men of the country. What we are banded together to fight is not a party, is not a great body of citizens; we have to fight only little coteries, groups of men here and there, a few men, who subsist by deceiving us and cannot subsist a moment after they cease to deceive us.

I had occasion to test the power of such a group in the State of New Jersey, and I had the satisfaction of discovering that I had been right in supposing that they did not possess any power at all. It looked as if they were entrenched in a fortress; it looked as if the embrasures of the fortress showed the muzzles of guns; but, as I told my good fellow-citizens, all they had to do was to press a little upon it and they would find that the fortress was a mere cardboard fabric; that it was a piece of stage property; that just so soon as the audience got ready to look behind the scenes they would learn that the army which had been marching and counter-marching in such terrifying array consisted of a single company that had gone in one wing and around and out at the other wing, and could have thus marched in procession for twenty-four hours. You only need about twenty-four men to do the trick. These men are impostors. They are powerful only in proportion as we are susceptible to absurd fear of them. Their capital is our ignorance and our credulity.

To-day we are seeing something that some of us have waited all of our lives to see. We are witnessing a rising of the country. We are seeing a whole people stand up and decline any longer to be imposed upon. The day has come when men are saying to each other: "It doesn't make a peppercorn's difference to me what party I have voted with. I am going to pick out the men I want and the policies I want, and let the label take care of itself. I do not find any great difference between my table of contents and the table of contents of those who have voted with the other party, and who, like me, are very much dissatisfied with the way in which their party has rewarded their faithfulness. They want the same things that I want, and I don't know of anything under God's heaven to prevent our getting together. We want the same things, we have the same faith in the old traditions of the American people, and we have made up our minds that we are going to have now at last the reality instead of the shadow."

We Americans have been too long satisfied with merely going through the motions of government. We have been having a mock game. We have been going to the polls and saying: "This is the act of a sovereign people, but we won't be the sovereign yet; we will postpone that; we will wait until another time. The managers are still shifting the scenes; we are not ready for the real thing yet."

My proposal is that we stop going through the mimic play; that we get out and translate the ideals of American politics into action; so that every man, when he goes to the polls on election day, will feel the thrill of executing an actual judgment, as he takes again into his own hands the great matters which have been too long left to men deputized by their own choice, and seriously sets about carrying into accomplishment his own purposes.

# XI

# THE EMANCIPATION OF BUSINESS

In the readjustments that are about to be undertaken in this country not one single legitimate or honest arrangement is going to be disturbed; but every impediment to business is going to be removed, every illegitimate kind of control is going to be destroyed. Every man who wants an opportunity and has the energy to seize it, is going to be given a chance. All that we are going to ask the gentlemen who now enjoy monopolistic advantages to do is to match their brains against the brains of those who will then compete with them. The brains, the energy, of the rest of us are to be set free to go into the game,—that is all. There is to be a general release of the capital, the enterprise, of millions of people, a general opening of the doors of opportunity. With what a spring of determination, with what a shout of jubilance, will the people rise to their emancipation!

I am one of those who believe that we have had such restrictions upon the prosperity of this country that we have not yet come into our own, and that by removing those restrictions we shall set free an energy which in our generation has not been known. It is for that reason that I feel free to criticise with the utmost frankness these restrictions, and the means by which they have been brought about. I do not criticise as one without hope; in describing conditions which so hamper, impede, and imprison, I am only describing conditions from which we are going to escape into a contrasting age. I believe that this is a time when there should be unqualified frankness. One of the distressing circumstances of our day is this: I cannot tell you how many men of business, how many important men of business, have communicated their real opinions about the situation in the United States to me privately and confidentially. They are afraid of somebody. They are afraid to make their real opinions known publicly; they tell them to me behind their hand. That is very distressing. That means that we are not masters of our own opinions, except when we vote, and even then we are careful to vote very privately indeed.

It is alarming that this should be the case. Why should any man in free America be afraid of any other man? Or why should any man fear competition,—competition either with his fellow-countrymen or with anybody else on earth?

It is part of the indictment against the protective policy of the United States that it has weakened and not enhanced the vigor of our people. American manufacturers who know that they can make better things than are made elsewhere in the world, that they can sell them cheaper in foreign markets than they are sold in these very markets of domestic manufacture, are afraid,—afraid to venture out into the great world on their own merits and their own skill. Think of it, a nation full of genius and yet paralyzed by timidity! The timidity of the business men of America is to me nothing less than amazing. They are tied to the apron strings of the government at Washington. They go about to seek favors. They say: "For pity's sake, don't expose us to the weather of the world; put some homelike cover over us. Protect us. See to it that foreign men don't come in and match their brains with ours." And, as if to enhance this peculiarity of ours, the strongest men amongst us get the biggest favors; the men of peculiar genius for organizing industries, the men who could run the industries of any country, are the men who are most strongly intrenched behind the highest rates in the schedules of the tariff. They are so timid morally, furthermore, that they dare not stand up before the American people, but conceal these favors in the verbiage of the tariff schedule itself,—in "jokers." Ah! but it is a bitter joke when men who seek favors are so afraid of the best judgment of their fellow-citizens that they dare not avow what they take.

Happily, the general revival of conscience in this country has not been confined to those who were consciously fighting special privilege. The awakening of conscience has extended to those who were *enjoying* special privileges, and I thank God that the business men of this country are beginning to see our economic organization in its true light, as a deadening aristocracy of privilege from which they themselves must escape. The small men of this country are not deluded, and not all of the big business men of this country are deluded. Some men who have been led into wrong practices, who have been led into the practices of monopoly, because that seemed to be the drift and inevitable method of supremacy, are just as ready as we are to turn about and adopt the process of freedom. For American hearts beat in a lot of these men, just as they beat under our jackets. They will be as glad to be free as we shall be to set them free. And then the splendid force which has lent itself to things that hurt us will lend itself to things that benefit us.

And we,—we who are not great captains of industry or business,—shall do them more good than we do now, even in a material way. If you have to be subservient, you are not even making the rich fellows as rich as they might be, because you are not adding your originative force to the extraordinary production of wealth in America. America is as rich, not as Wall Street, not as the financial centres in Chicago and St. Louis and San Francisco; it is as rich as the people that make those centres rich. And if those people hesitate in their enterprise, cower in the face of power, hesitate to originate designs of their own, then the very fountains which make these places abound in wealth are dried up at the source. By setting the little men of America free, you are not damaging the giants.

It may be that certain things will happen, for monopoly in this country is carrying a body of water such as men ought not to be asked to carry. When by regulated competition,—that is to say, fair competition, competition that fights fair,—they are put upon their mettle, they will have to economize, and they cannot economize unless they get rid of that water. I do not know how to squeeze the water out, but they will get rid of it, if you will put them to the necessity. They will have to get rid of it, or those of us who don't carry tanks will outrun them in the race. Put all the business of America upon the footing of economy and efficiency, and then let the race be to the strongest and the swiftest.

Our program is a program of prosperity; a program of prosperity that is to be a little more pervasive than the present prosperity,—and pervasive prosperity is more fruitful than that which is narrow and restrictive. I congratulate the monopolies of the United States that they are not going to have their way, because, quite contrary to their own theory, the fact is that the people are wiser than they are. The people of the United States understand the United States as these gentlemen do not, and if they will only give us leave, we will not only make them rich, but we will make them happy. Because, then, their conscience will have less to carry. I have lived in a state that was owned by a series of corporations. They handed it about. It was at one time owned by the Pennsylvania Railroad; then it was owned by the Public Service Corporation. It was owned by the Public Service

Corporation when I was admitted, and that corporation has been resentful ever since that I interfered with its tenancy. But I really did not see any reason why the people should give up their own residence to so small a body of men to monopolize; and, therefore, when I asked them for their title deeds and they couldn't produce them, and there was no court except the court of public opinion to resort to, they moved out. Now they eat out of our hands; and they are not losing flesh either. They are making just as much money as they made before, only they are making it in a more respectable way. They are making it without the constant assistance of the legislature of the State of New Jersey. They are making it in the normal way, by supplying the people of New Jersey with the service in the way of transportation and gas and water that they really need. I do not believe that there are any thoughtful officials of the Public Service Corporation of New Jersey that now seriously regret the change that has come about. We liberated government in my state, and it is an interesting fact that we have not suffered one moment in prosperity.

---

What we propose, therefore, in this program of freedom, is a program of general advantage. Almost every monopoly that has resisted dissolution has resisted the real interests of its own stockholders. Monopoly always checks development, weighs down natural prosperity, pulls against natural advance.

Take but such an everyday thing as a useful invention and the putting of it at the service of men. You know how prolific the American mind has been in invention; how much civilization has been advanced by the steamboat, the cotton-gin, the sewing-machine, the reaping-machine, the typewriter, the electric light, the telephone, the phonograph. Do you know, have you had occasion to learn, that there is no hospitality for invention nowadays? There is no encouragement for you to set your wits at work to improve the telephone, or the camera, or some piece of machinery, or some mechanical process; you are not invited to find a shorter and cheaper way to make things or to perfect them, or to invent better things to take their place. There is too much money invested in old machinery; too much money has been spent advertising the old camera; the telephone plants, as they are, cost too much to permit their being superseded by something better. Wherever there is monopoly, not only is there no incentive to improve, but, improvement being costly in that it "scraps" old machinery and destroys the value of old products, there is a positive motive against improvement. The instinct of monopoly is against novelty, the tendency of monopoly is to keep in use the old thing, made in the old way; its disposition is to "standardize" everything. Standardization may be all very well,—but suppose everything had been standardized thirty years ago,—we should still be writing by hand, by gas-light, we should be without the inestimable aid of the telephone (sometimes, I admit, it is a nuisance), without the automobile, without wireless telegraphy. Personally, I could have managed to plod along without the aeroplane, and I could have been happy even without moving-pictures.

Of course, I am not saying that all invention has been stopped by the growth of trusts, but I think it is perfectly clear that invention in many fields has been discouraged, that inventors have been prevented from reaping the full fruits of their ingenuity and industry, and that mankind has been deprived of many comforts and conveniences, as well as of the opportunity of buying at lower prices.

The damper put on the inventive genius of America by the trusts operates in half a dozen ways: The first thing discovered by the genius whose device extends into a field controlled by a trust is that he can't get capital to make and market his invention. If you want money to build your plant and advertise your product and employ your agents and make a market for it, where are you going to get it? The minute you apply for money or credit, this proposition is put to you by the banks: "This invention will interfere with the established processes and the market control of certain great industries. We are already financing those industries, their securities are in our hands; we will consult them."

It may be, as a result of that consultation, you will be informed that it is too bad, but it will be impossible to "accommodate" you. It may be you will receive a suggestion that if you care to make certain arrangements with the trust, you will be permitted to manufacture. It may be you will receive an offer to buy your patent, the offer being a poor consolation dole. It may be that your invention, even if purchased, will never be heard of again.

That last method of dealing with an invention, by the way, is a particularly vicious misuse of the patent laws, which ought not to allow property in an idea which is never intended to be realized. One of the reforms waiting to be undertaken is a revision of our patent laws.

In any event, if the trust doesn't want you to manufacture your invention, you will not be allowed to, unless you have money of your own and are willing to risk it fighting the monopolistic trust with its vast resources. I am generalizing the statement, but I could particularize it. I could tell you instances where exactly that thing happened. By the combination of great industries, manufactured products are not only being standardized, but they are too often being kept at a single point of development and efficiency. The increase of the power to produce in proportion to the cost of production is not studied in America as it used to be studied, because if you don't have to improve your processes in order to excel a competitor, if you are human you aren't going to improve your processes; and if you can prevent the competitor from coming into the field, then you can sit at your leisure, and, behind this wall of protection which prevents the brains of any foreigner competing with you, you can rest at your ease for a whole generation.

Can any one who reflects on merely this attitude of the trusts toward invention fail to understand how substantial, how actual, how great will be the effect of the release of the genius of our people to originate, improve, and perfect the instruments and circumstances of our lives? Who can say what patents now lying, unrealized, in secret drawers and pigeonholes, will come to light, or what new inventions will astonish and bless us, when freedom is restored?

Are you not eager for the time when the genius and initiative of all the people shall be called into the service of business? when newcomers with new ideas, new entries with new enthusiasms, independent men, shall be welcomed? when your sons shall be able to look forward to becoming, not employees, but heads of some small, it may be, but hopeful, business, where their best energies shall be inspired by the knowledge that they are their own masters, with the paths of the world open before them? Have you no desire to see the markets opened to all? to see credit available in due proportion to every man of character and serious purpose who can use it safely and to advantage? to see business disentangled from its unholy alliance with politics? to see raw material released from the control of monopolists, and transportation facilities equalized for all? and every avenue of commercial and industrial activity levelled for the feet of all who would tread it? Surely, you must feel the inspiration of such a new dawn of liberty!

---

There is the great policy of conservation, for example; and I do not conceive of conservation in any narrow sense. There are forests to conserve, there are great water powers to conserve, there are mines whose wealth should be deemed exhaustible, not inexhaustible, and whose resources should be safeguarded and preserved for future generations. But there is much more. There are the lives and energies of the people to be physically safeguarded.

You know what has been the embarrassment about conservation. The federal government has not dared relax its hold, because, not *bona fide* settlers, not men bent upon the legitimate development of great states, but men bent upon getting into their own exclusive control great mineral, forest, and water resources, have stood at the ear of the government and attempted to dictate its policy. And the government of the United States has not dared relax its somewhat rigid policy because of the fear that these forces would be stronger than the forces of individual communities and of the public interest. What we are now in dread of is that this situation will be made permanent. Why is it that Alaska has lagged in her development? Why is it that there are great mountains of coal piled up in the shipping places on the coast of Alaska which the government at Washington will not permit to be sold? It is because the government is not sure that it has followed all the intricate threads of intrigue by which small bodies of men have tried to get exclusive control of the coal fields of Alaska. The government stands itself suspicious of the forces by which it is surrounded.

The trouble about conservation is that the government of the United States hasn't any policy at present. It is simply marking time. It is simply standing still. Reservation is not conservation. Simply to say, "We are not going to do anything about the forests," when the country needs to use the forests, is not a practicable program at all. To say that the people of the great State of Washington can't buy coal out of the Alaskan coal fields doesn't settle the question. You have got to have that coal sooner or later. And if you are so afraid of the Guggenheims and all the rest of them that you can't make up your mind what your policies are going to be about those coal fields, how long are we going to wait for the government to throw off its fear? There can't be a working program until there is a free government. The day when the government is free to set about a policy of positive conservation, as distinguished from mere negative reservation, will be an emancipation day of no small importance for the development of the country.

But the question of conservation is a very much bigger question than the conservation of our natural resources; because in summing up our natural resources there is one great natural resource which underlies them all, and seems to underlie them so deeply that we sometimes overlook it. I mean the people themselves.

What would our forests be worth without vigorous and intelligent men to make use of them? Why should we conserve our natural resources, unless we can by the magic of industry transmute them into the wealth of the world? What transmutes them into that wealth, if not the skill and the touch of the men who go daily to their toil and who constitute the great body of the American people? What I am interested in is having the government of the United States more concerned about human rights than about property rights. Property is an instrument of humanity; humanity isn't an instrument of property. And yet when you see some men riding their great industries as if they were driving a car of juggernaut, not looking to see what multitudes prostrate themselves before the car and lose their lives in the crushing effect of their industry, you wonder how long men are going to be permitted to think more of their machinery than they think of their men. Did you never think of it,—men are cheap, and machinery is dear; many a superintendent is dismissed for overdriving a delicate machine, who wouldn't be dismissed for overdriving an overtaxed man. You can discard your man and replace him; there are others ready to come into his place; but you can't without great cost discard your machine and put a new one in its place. You are less apt, therefore, to look upon your men as the essential vital foundation part of your whole business. It is time that property, as compared with humanity, should take second place, not first place. We must see to it that there is no over-crowding, that there is no bad sanitation, that there is no unnecessary spread of avoidable diseases, that the purity of food is safeguarded, that there is every precaution against accident, that women are not driven to impossible tasks, nor children permitted to spend their energy before it is fit to be spent. The hope and elasticity of the race must be preserved; men must be preserved according to their individual needs, and not according to the programs of industry merely. What is the use of having industry, if we perish in producing it? If we die in trying to feed ourselves, why should we eat? If we die trying to get a foothold in the crowd, why not let the crowd trample us sooner and be done with it? I tell you that there is beginning to beat in this nation a great pulse of irresistible sympathy which is going to transform the processes of government amongst us. The strength of America is proportioned only to the health, the energy, the hope, the elasticity, the buoyancy of the American people.

Is not that the greatest thought that you can have of freedom,—the thought of it as a gift that shall release men and women from all that pulls them back from being their best and from doing their best, that shall liberate their energy to its fullest limit, free their aspirations till no bounds confine them, and fill their spirits with the jubilance of realizable hope?

# XII

# THE LIBERATION OF A PEOPLE'S VITAL ENERGIES

No matter how often we think of it, the discovery of America must each time make a fresh appeal to our imaginations. For centuries, indeed from the beginning, the face of Europe had been turned toward the east. All the routes of trade, every impulse and energy, ran from west to east. The Atlantic lay at the world's back-door. Then, suddenly, the conquest of Constantinople by the Turk closed the route to the Orient. Europe had either to face about or lack any outlet for her energies; the unknown sea at the west at last was ventured upon, and the earth learned that it was twice as big as it had thought. Columbus did not find, as he had expected, the civilization of Cathay; he found an empty continent. In that part of the world, upon that new-found half of the globe, mankind, late in its history, was thus afforded an opportunity to set up a new civilization; here it was strangely privileged to make a new human experiment.

Never can that moment of unique opportunity fail to excite the emotion of all who consider its strangeness and richness; a thousand fanciful histories of the earth might be contrived without the imagination daring to conceive such a romance as the hiding away of half the globe until the fulness of time had come for a new start in civilization. A mere sea captain's ambition to trace a new trade route gave way to a moral adventure for humanity. The race was to found a new order here on this delectable land, which no man approached without receiving, as the old voyagers relate, you remember, sweet airs out of woods aflame with flowers and murmurous with the sound of pellucid waters. The hemisphere lay waiting to be touched with life,— life from the old centres of living, surely, but cleansed of defilement, and cured of weariness, so as to be fit for the virgin purity of a new bride. The whole thing springs into the imagination like a wonderful vision, an exquisite marvel which once only in all history could be vouchsafed.

One other thing only compares with it; only one other thing touches the springs of emotion as does the picture of the ships of Columbus drawing near the bright shores,—and that is the thought of the choke in the throat of the immigrant of to-day as he gazes from the steerage deck at the land where he has been taught to believe he in his turn shall find an earthly paradise, where, a free man, he shall forget the heartaches of the old life, and enter into the fulfilment of the hope of the world. For has not every ship that has pointed her prow westward borne hither the hopes of generation after generation of the oppressed of other lands? How always have men's hearts beat as they saw the coast of America rise to their view! How it has always seemed to them that the dweller there would at last be rid of kings, of privileged classes, and of all those bonds which had kept men depressed and helpless, and would there realize the full fruition of his sense of honest manhood, would there be one of a great body of brothers, not seeking to defraud and deceive one another, but seeking to accomplish the general good!

What was in the writings of the men who founded America,—to serve the selfish interests of America? Do you find that in their writings? No; to serve the cause of humanity, to bring liberty to mankind. They set up their standards here in America in the tenet of hope, as a beacon of encouragement to all the nations of the world; and men came thronging to these shores with an expectancy that never existed before, with a confidence they never dared feel before, and found here for generations together a haven of peace, of opportunity, of equality.

God send that in the complicated state of modern affairs we may recover the standards and repeat the achievements of that heroic age!

For life is no longer the comparatively simple thing it was. Our relations one with another have been profoundly modified by the new agencies of rapid communication and transportation, tending swiftly to concentrate life, widen communities, fuse interests, and complicate all the processes of living. The individual is dizzily swept about in a thousand new whirlpools of activities. Tyranny has become more subtle, and has learned to wear the guise of mere industry, and even of benevolence. Freedom has become a somewhat different matter. It cannot,—eternal principle that it is,—it cannot have altered, yet it shows itself in new aspects. Perhaps it is only revealing its deeper meaning.

What is liberty?

I have long had an image in my mind of what constitutes liberty. Suppose that I were building a great piece of powerful machinery, and suppose that I should so awkwardly and unskilfully assemble the parts of it that every time one part tried to move it would be interfered with by the others, and the whole thing would buckle up and be checked. Liberty for the several parts would consist in the best possible assembling and adjustment of them all, would it not? If you want the great piston of the engine to run with absolute freedom, give it absolutely perfect alignment and adjustment with the other parts of the machine, so that it is free, not because it is let alone or isolated, but because it has been associated most skilfully and carefully with the other parts of the great structure.

What it liberty? You say of the locomotive that it runs free. What do you mean? You mean that its parts are so assembled and adjusted that friction is reduced to a minimum, and that it has perfect adjustment. We say of a boat skimming the water with light foot, "How free she runs," when we mean, how perfectly she is adjusted to the force of the wind, how perfectly she obeys the great breath out of the heavens that fills her sails. Throw her head up into the wind and see how she will halt and stagger, how every sheet will shiver and her whole frame be shaken, how instantly she is "in irons," in the expressive phrase of the sea. She is free only when you have let her fall off again and have recovered once more her nice adjustment to the forces she must obey and cannot defy.

Human freedom consists in perfect adjustments of human interests and human activities and human energies.

Now, the adjustments necessary between individuals, between individuals and the complex institutions amidst which they live, and between those institutions and the government, are infinitely more intricate to-day than ever before. No doubt this is a tiresome and roundabout way of saying the thing, yet perhaps it is worth while to get somewhat clearly in our mind what makes all the trouble to-day. Life has become complex; there are many more elements, more parts, to it than ever before. And, therefore, it is harder to keep everything adjusted,—and harder to find out where the trouble lies when the machine gets out of order.

You know that one of the interesting things that Mr. Jefferson said in those early days of simplicity which marked the beginnings of our government was that the best government consisted in as little governing as possible. And there is still a sense in which that is true. It is still intolerable for the government to interfere with our individual activities except where it is necessary to interfere with them in order to free them. But I feel confident that if Jefferson were living in our day he would see what we see: that the individual is caught in a great confused nexus of all sorts of complicated circumstances, and that to let him alone is to leave him helpless as against the obstacles with which he has to contend; and that, therefore, law in our day must come to the assistance of the individual. It must come to his assistance to see that he gets fair play; that is all, but that is much. Without the watchful interference, the resolute interference, of the government, there can be no fair play between individuals and such powerful institutions as the trusts. Freedom to-day is something more than being let alone. The program of a government of freedom must in these days be positive, not negative merely.

---

Well, then, in this new sense and meaning of it, are we preserving freedom in this land of ours, the hope of all the earth?

Have we, inheritors of this continent and of the ideals to which the fathers consecrated it,—have we maintained them, realizing them, as each generation must, anew? Are we, in the consciousness that the life of man is pledged to higher levels here than elsewhere, striving still to bear aloft the standards of liberty and hope, or, disillusioned and defeated, are we feeling the disgrace of having had a free field in which to do new things and of not having done them?

The answer must be, I am sure, that we have been in a fair way of failure,— tragic failure. And we stand in danger of utter failure yet except we fulfil speedily the determination we have reached, to deal with the new and subtle tyrannies according to their deserts. Don't deceive yourselves for a moment as to the power of the great interests which now dominate our development. They are so great that it is almost an open question whether the government of the United States can dominate them or not. Go one step further, make their organized power permanent, and it may be too late to turn back. The roads diverge at the point where we stand. They stretch their vistas out to regions where they are very far separated from one another; at the end of one is the old tiresome scene of government tied up with special interests; and at the other shines the liberating light of individual initiative, of individual liberty, of individual freedom, the light of untrammeled enterprise. I believe that that light shines out of the heavens itself that God has created. I believe in human liberty as I believe in the wine of life. There is no salvation for men in the pitiful condescensions of industrial masters. Guardians have no place in a land of freemen. Prosperity guaranteed by trustees has no prospect of endurance. Monopoly means the atrophy of enterprise. If monopoly persists, monopoly will always sit at the helm of the government. I do not expect to see monopoly restrain itself. If there are men in this country big enough to own the government of the United States, they are going to own it; what we have to determine now is whether we are big enough, whether we are men enough, whether we are free enough, to take possession again of the government which is our own. We haven't had free access to it, our minds have not touched it by way of guidance, in half a generation, and now we are engaged in nothing less than the recovery of what was made with our own hands, and acts only by our delegated authority.

I tell you, when you discuss the question of the tariffs and of the trusts, you are discussing the very lives of yourselves and your children. I believe that I am preaching the very cause of some of the gentlemen whom I am opposing when I preach the cause of free industry in the United States, for I think they are slowly girding the tree that bears the inestimable fruits of our life, and that if they are permitted to gird it entirely nature will take her revenge and the tree will die.

I do not believe that America is securely great because she has great men in her now. America is great in proportion as she can make sure of having great men in the next generation. She is rich in her unborn children; rich, that is to say, if those unborn children see the sun in a day of opportunity, see the sun when they are free to exercise their energies as they will. If they open their eyes in a land where there is no special privilege, then we shall come into a new era of American greatness and American liberty; but if they open their eyes in a country where they must be employees or nothing, if they open their eyes in a land of merely regulated monopoly, where all the conditions of industry are determined by small groups of men, then they will see an America such as the founders of this Republic would have wept to think of. The only hope is in the release of the forces which philanthropic trust presidents want to monopolize. Only the emancipation, the freeing and heartening of the vital energies of all the people will redeem us. In all that I may have to do in public affairs in the United States I am going to think of towns such as I have seen in Indiana, towns of the old American pattern, that own and operate their own industries, hopefully and happily. My thought is going to be bent upon the multiplication of towns of that kind and the prevention of the concentration of industry in this country in such a fashion and upon such a scale that towns that own themselves will be impossible. You know what the vitality of America consists of. Its vitality does not lie in New York, nor in Chicago; it will not be sapped by anything that happens in St. Louis. The vitality of America lies in the brains, the energies, the enterprise of the people throughout the land; in the efficiency of their factories and in the richness of the fields that stretch beyond the borders of the town; in the wealth which they extract from nature and originate for themselves through the inventive genius characteristic of all free American communities.

That is the wealth of America, and if America discourages the locality, the community, the self-contained town, she will kill the nation. A nation is as rich as her free communities; she is not as rich as her capital city or her metropolis. The amount of money in Wall Street is no indication of the wealth of the American people. That indication can be found only in the fertility of the American mind and the productivity of American industry everywhere throughout the United States. If America were not rich and fertile, there would be no money in Wall Street. If Americans were not vital and able to take care of themselves, the great money exchanges would break down. The welfare, the very existence of the nation, rests at last upon the great mass of the people; its prosperity depends at last upon the spirit in which they go about their work in their several communities throughout the broad land. In proportion as her towns and her country-sides are happy and hopeful will America realize the high ambitions which have marked her in the eyes of all the world.

The welfare, the happiness, the energy and spirit of the men and women who do the daily work in our mines and factories, on our railroads, in our offices and ports of trade, on our farms and on the sea, is the underlying necessity of all prosperity. There can be nothing wholesome unless their life is wholesome; there can be no contentment unless they are contented. Their physical welfare affects the soundness of the whole nation. How would it suit the prosperity of the United States, how would it suit business, to have a people that went every day sadly or sullenly to their work? How would the future look to you if you felt that the aspiration had gone out of most men, the confidence of success, the hope that they might improve their condition? Do you not see that just so soon as the old self-confidence of America, just so soon as her old boasted advantage of individual liberty and opportunity, is taken away, all the energy of her people begins to subside, to slacken, to grow loose and pulpy, without fibre, and men simply cast about to see that the day does not end disastrously with them?

So we must put heart into the people by taking the heartlessness out of politics, business, and industry. We have got to make politics a thing in which an honest man can take his part with satisfaction because he knows that his opinion will count as much as the next man's, and that the boss and the interests have been dethroned. Business we have got to untrammel, abolishing tariff favors, and railroad discrimination, and credit denials, and all forms of unjust handicaps against the little man. Industry we have got to humanize,—not through the trusts,—but through the direct action of law guaranteeing protection against dangers and compensation for injuries, guaranteeing sanitary conditions, proper hours, the right to organize, and all the other things which the conscience of the country demands as the workingman's right. We have got to cheer and inspirit our people with the sure prospects of social justice and due reward, with the vision of the open gates of opportunity for all. We have got to set the energy and the initiative of this great people absolutely free, so that the future of America will be greater than the past, so that the pride of America will grow with achievement, so that America will know as she advances from generation to generation that each brood of her sons is greater and more enlightened than that which preceded it, know that she is fulfilling the promise that she has made to mankind.

Such is the vision of some of us who now come to assist in its realization. For we Democrats would not have endured this long burden of exile if we had not seen a vision. We could have traded; we could have got into the game; we could have surrendered and made terms; we could have played the rôle of patrons to the men who wanted to dominate the interests of the country,—and here and there gentlemen who pretended to be of us did make those arrangements. They couldn't stand privation. You never can stand it unless you have within you some imperishable food upon which to sustain life and courage, the food of those visions of the spirit where a table is set before us laden with palatable fruits, the fruits of hope, the fruits of imagination, those invisible things of the spirit which are the only things upon which we can sustain ourselves through this weary world without fainting. We have carried in our minds, after you had thought you had obscured and blurred them, the ideals of those men who first set their foot upon America, those little bands who came to make a foothold in the wilderness, because the great teeming nations that they had left behind them had forgotten what human liberty was, liberty of thought, liberty of religion, liberty of residence, liberty of action.

Since their day the meaning of liberty has deepened. But it has not ceased to be a fundamental demand of the human spirit, a fundamental necessity for the life of the soul. And the day is at hand when it shall be realized on this consecrated soil,—a New Freedom,—a Liberty widened and deepened to match the broadened life of man in modern America, restoring to him in very truth the control of his government, throwing wide all gates of lawful enterprise, unfettering his energies, and warming the generous impulses of his heart,—a process of release, emancipation, and inspiration, full of a breath of life as sweet and wholesome as the airs that filled the sails of the caravels of Columbus and gave the promise and boast of magnificent Opportunity in which America *dare not fail.*

www.ingramcontent.com/pod-product-compliance
Lightning Source LLC
Chambersburg PA
CBHW081619100526
44590CB00021B/3504